THE COMPLETE

Sports Massage

Tim Paine

A & C Black • London

To my mother and father, for their unceasing love and support,
and my wife Fid for her endless patience.

Published in 2000 by A & C Black (Publishers) Ltd
35 Bedford Row, London WC1R 4JH

Copyright © 2000 by Tim Paine

Reprinted 2000

ISBN 0 7136 5007 9

A CIP catalogue record for this book
is available from the British Library

Illustration acknowledgements
Cover photograph by Graham Watson
Textual photography by Shane Gunning
Illustrations by Jean Ashley, Ron Dixon of Typetech
and Dave Saunders: Figs 3.1, 3.2, 3.3, 3.7 and 7.2 from
The Complete Guide to Stretching by Christopher M.
Norris; Fig. 3.4 from *Black's Medical Dictionary;* Figs
3.5, 4.1 and 7.3 from *Abdominal Training* by
Christopher M. Norris; Fig. 3.6 from *The Complete
Guide to Exercise to Music* by Debbie Lawrence

Typeset in 10½ on 12pt Palatino

Printed and bound in Great Britain by
Biddles Ltd, Guildford and King's Lynn

Contents

Acknowledgements

♦ Brian Webster MCSP, whom I have tutored with for some years and whose knowledge constantly reminds me of how much more there is to learn.

♦ The many sports massage students whom I have had the pleasure to work with.

♦ Stephanie Croxton, David Heard and Brian Fuller for reading each chapter, expressing their views and adding their expertise. Also Dr Michael Benjamin, senior anatomist at Cardiff University, for his invaluable advice on Chapter 3, and Peter Sheard, who provided technical expertise in several areas of this book.

♦ Colleagues at the Academy of Sports Therapy for their support in helping me complete this book.

♦ The players at Finchley RFC for allowing me to work with them, and for the superb camaraderie I have enjoyed with them.

Introduction

With more and more people participating in an increasing number of sports at all levels, there is a growing demand for professionally trained people who offer a variety of sport-related skills. Massage has been used for thousands of years and in recent decades has re-emerged as an accepted method to enhance the physical, physiological and psychological wellbeing of the active person.

As you will discover in this book, the demands placed upon the professional sports massage therapist are many. In your day to day work you will be required to practise in a number of settings and draw on a wide base of knowledge. You will also be required to appreciate the workings of the human body, understand the effects of exercise and the benefits of massage, and to undertake a sound training and extensive practise in order to perfect your skills.

Having decided to enter the field of sports massage *The Complete Guide to Sports Massage* will provide much of the information needed to accompany your training. From the science of sports massage to the much broader range of skills required for you to help your clients, you will gain much of the knowledge and practical skill required to help you qualify and start a successful practice.

Tim Paine
July 2000

PART ONE

About sports massage

Chapter 1

An introduction to sports massage

◆ What is sports massage ◆

Sports massage is a form of massage involving the manipulation of *soft tissue* to benefit a person engaged in regular physical activity. Soft tissue is connective tissue that has not hardened into bone and cartilage and includes skin, muscles, tendons, ligaments and fascia (a form of connective tissue that lines and ensheathes the other soft tissues). Sports massage is designed to assist in correcting problems and imbalances in soft tissue that are caused from repetitive and strenuous physical activity and trauma. The application of sports massage, prior to and after exercise, may enhance performance, aid recovery and prevent injury.

◆ Where did sports massage ◆ originate?

Massage is recorded as one of the earliest forms of physical therapy and was used over 3000 years ago in China, India and Greece. Its popular use in the Western world is largely due to the work of Per Henrik Ling (1776–1839), who developed the form of massage now known as *Swedish massage*. Ling developed his own style of massage and exercise to help fencers and gymnasts, gaining international recognition in the process. Many of his ideas have formed the foundations of modern sports massage. Today, there are many forms of massage available to assist us in maintaining our health and wellbeing. Sports massage has been accepted in America, Canada and Australia for many years now, while in the UK, the practice only became known and more widely used in the 1990s. Very few courses were available until then (*see* also p. 3).

1

♦ The benefits of sports ♦ massage

How does sports massage benefit people who exercise?

Sports massage benefits people who exercise by assisting in the processes of *over-compensation* and *adaptation*. During and after exercise, the body's systems adapt to cope with the increased stresses placed on them. These adaptations affect the muscles, the bones, the tissues, the nerves and the brain. In the right measure and at the right frequency, regular exercise enables the body to cope with increased levels of stress (overload), which allows the body to exercise at higher intensities or for longer durations. This is possible because of a process called overcompensation. While the body is recovering from overload as a result of exercise, the body overcompensates to increase its power of resistance to future stress.

How the body overcompensates or adapts to exercise depends on the type of stress placed on it. Training programmes for fitness or sport are based on the principle of *specificity*, which states that the adaptations will be specific to the type of stress. For example, a soccer player, who requires bursts of explosive power over short distances, will need a training programme that includes specific exercises to improve speed. On the other hand, a marathon runner, who requires a high level of aerobic efficiency to complete the long distance, needs a training programme that focuses on improving endurance.

The manipulation of soft tissue prior to and after exercise promotes physical, physiological and psychological changes that aid performance and particularly recovery. Some examples of the benefits for the exerciser are:

♦ the release of muscle tension and pain;
♦ the removal of waste products such as acetic acid and carbon dioxide;
♦ reduced discomfort from DOMS (delayed onset muscle soreness) as a result of vigorous exercise;
♦ and improved posture and flexibility.

Further details on the effects of exercise and sports massage on the body, and on how sports massage can aid the exerciser (hereafter referred to as the 'athlete'), are explained in Part Two of this book, *The science of sports massage*.

Who can benefit from sports massage?

Anyone who engages in physical activity for the purpose of sport or fitness – irrespective of age, level of fitness or level of training – can benefit. Athletes with injuries or problems that are inhibiting performance will find that the stimulatory effects of sports massage encourage the healing process. Recreational and competitive athletes following a regular training programme will benefit during recovery, and through the early detection of any problems arising from training stress. Athletes engaged in sporting events or competitions can benefit before, during and after the event, depending on whether the need is for the release of muscle tension, relief from soreness, relaxation, etc.

♦ Sports massage and ♦ sports therapy

Sports massage is one of the skills utilised in the practice of sports therapy. In addition to massage, sports therapy also includes the management and treatment of sports injuries, exercise therapy and rehabilitation, and sports nutrition.

◆ Is sports massage a ◆ recognised form of therapy?

Sports massage has become more popular as the number of people participating in sport and fitness and the physical demands placed on athletes has increased. Many athletes are being introduced to sports massage and are increasingly aware of the benefits. While it is a recognised practice in the United States, Canada, Australia and some European countries as mentioned above, acceptance in the UK has been a slow process. In addition, a lack of scientific evidence to support the anecdotal benefits of sports massage has hindered its development.

Research in sports medicine, however, is revealing more information about the effects of exercise and injury on the human body and its systems, which can now be utilised in the study of sports massage. As a result, sports massage is becoming more widely accepted by athletes, sports scientists, coaches and industry bodies as a means of enhancing performance, aiding recovery and preventing injury.

While there is currently no national governing body responsible for setting professional standards of practice for sports massage, the National Sports Medicine Institute has formed a committee to draw up minimum criteria for the teaching of sports massage. A register of teaching organisations that meet these criteria has now been established for the public: this is available through the National Sports Medicine Institute (*see* p. 165).

◆ How is sports massage ◆ different from other massage?

While other forms of massage, such as Swedish or holistic massage, have some aims in common with sports massage – such as physical and mental relaxation – sports massage is specifically designed to assist athletes in their sport or fitness activities. A sports massage therapist is concerned primarily with:

◆ muscular and skeletal alignment;
◆ how exercise affects the body's systems;
◆ and how massage can promote or reduce these effects to the benefit of the athlete.

Many of the aims of sports massage, such as injury prevention and the promotion of recovery from exercise, are therefore quite different from the aims of other forms of massage.

◆ When is sports massage ◆ contraindicated?

Contraindications are circumstances in which sports massage might or would be detrimental to an athlete's health and wellbeing, so it is vital to know what they are and understand how to assess them.

The sports massage therapist must ask about some contraindications prior to starting, as a preliminary check. Others will become evident if present, by observation and palpation (*see* Chapter 8, pp. 74–6) during the treatment session. Once you have asked your questions, a good way to complete your history-taking is to verbally summarise your client's history and then add: 'Are there any injuries or conditions that we have not yet covered, and are you taking any medication that you have not yet told me about?' This is all-encompassing and will prompt your client to tell you about anything which might have been missed. If the client does have a condition which may be contraindicated, and you feel that they should be referred back to their GP, try to raise the subject tactfully and without alarming them. Reassure them by saying that you are not medically trained, and it would be wise to have a GP check this for you.

Sports massage can be contraindicated in any of the following circumstances.

When the client has a temperature over 100°F, or is feeling unwell

In these circumstances, the onset of illness may be accelerated by massage. If there is an excess of toxins in the body that is causing the client to feel unwell, both exercise and massage will increase the circulation of these toxins and exacerbate the condition. It is therefore advisable to refrain from both exercise and massage to allow the body's own defence mechanisms time to deal with the infection and to recover.

Acute traumas

Open wounds, recent bruising, muscle tears, sprained ligaments, contusions, chilblains and burns must be avoided during their acute healing phases. During this phase, the damaged soft tissue will be in the early stages of healing and susceptible to further trauma if recently healed blood vessels are reopened by massage. For further information about soft tissue healing and injury management, *see* Chapter 12.

Skin infections

Look for any sign of skin infections on the surface of the skin such as swelling, redness, heat or pain. Any attempt to massage in the vicinity of these areas may spread the condition. The infection may also be passed on to you and possibly others.

Tumours

Where there is swelling which is inconsistent with recent bruising, avoid this area until you know what the cause is. If in doubt, advise the client to check with their doctor. This may be a tumour, which is an abnormal mass of tissue. If the tumour is malignant – a term used to describe a condition getting progressively worse, and spreading – massage may encourage the spread to secondary sites.

Diseased blood vessels

Phlebitis
Phlebitis refers to a condition of inflamed veins, often accompanied by blood clots (*see* below).

Thrombosis
A thrombosis is a blood clot, commonly occurring in the deep veins of the back of the legs where it is known as a *deep-vein thrombosis*. When a thrombosis is dislodged, it can have serious – and even fatal – consequences if it reaches the heart or lungs. This is a condition that is usually predisposed by a number of factors, including: a period of prolonged bed rest, varicose veins, an impact injury or heart disease. The condition may be detected by using the following as a guide: when you apply pressure to the area you will feel particularly firm swelling in a localised area, and the client will experience pain.

There may also be some swelling or discolouration distally – below the site – as blood collects behind the thrombosis.

Varicose veins
See below.

When the patient reacts adversely to treatment

If a person reacts adversely to treatment and there is no apparent reason, stop the massage and seek advice. In such cases the usual effects of massage may be detrimental.

Undiagnosed symptoms

If you encounter signs or symptoms of a condition you are not sure of, ask your client to obtain permission from their doctor for sports massage therapy. Be tactful when broaching the subject with your client so you don't alarm them unnecessarily.

The following conditions need not necessarily be contraindicated but do require considerable caution before the therapist proceeds. They are therefore shown separately.

Pregnancy

If you are massaging someone who is pregnant, extra care should be taken during the first 16 weeks, and the areas of the abdomen and lower back must be avoided during this time. If your client has experienced any problems or sickness during the early stages of pregnancy, ask them to seek permission to receive sports massage from their doctor. In the latter stages of pregnancy, finding a comfortable position for your client for their massage may be the only problem you encounter. (Special couches are made for this purpose.) Some women find massage beneficial in removing oedema (or swelling) around the ankles, and relieving aches in the lower back.

Diabetes

Diabetes is not contraindicated if it is properly managed. If your client is able to exercise they are unlikely to suffer any adverse reaction to massage. However, since massage stimulates blood circulation, blood sugar levels may be affected and your client should be aware of this so that they can adjust their medication accordingly.

Varicose veins

Varicose veins occur when valves in the veins fail and prevent the flow of blood back to the heart; this causes a pooling of blood, commonly in the legs. If someone has varicose veins that could be damaged by massage they will usually be under medical supervision and possibly awaiting surgery, so a simple check with your client will give you the information you need. If they are able to exercise, light effleurage (*see* Chapter 9, pp. 81–2 for information on this technique) properly applied in the direction of the heart is generally harmless. Varicose veins should not be confused, particularly after exercise, with blood vessels that have become prominent due to physical exertion.

5

Chapter 2

The sports massage therapist

Becoming a good sports massage therapist requires dedication, hard work, sound knowledge of the areas described below, and plenty of practice. Most people who embark on this form of training already have a keen interest in sport or rigorous physical activity. While you do not need qualifications to start with, you will need to learn anatomy and physiology, become confident at 'touching and handling' your clients, and be a good communicator.

◆ What a sports massage ◆ therapist needs to know

A sports massage therapist requires a wide range of knowledge and practical skills covering the following:

◆ anatomy and physiology;
◆ the effects of exercise on the human body and its systems;
◆ the physical, physiological and psychological effects of massage;
◆ how sports massage works to aid the athlete;
◆ how to assess problems;
◆ massage techniques and how to apply them to each part of the body;
◆ stretching techniques;
◆ first aid;
◆ injury management;
◆ safety in sport and exercise.

This book covers all these areas in detail to assist the student or new practitioner of sports massage. The information is also useful reference for those athletes, coaches and other industry professionals who wish to know more about how sports massage can aid performance and prevent injury.

As discussed early in Chapter 1, the sports massage therapist is concerned with the manipulation of soft tissues. It is important to recognise how much the sports massage therapist must know – and indeed, how much they are expected to carry out under professional practice. While they must be skilled in assessing a client's physical condition (*see* also Chapter 7), there is a line to be drawn between this and the diagnosis of traumatic injury and other conditions. This requires more extensive training and is often the realm of the medical practitioner or physiotherapist. If in any doubt, the client should always be referred on to an appropriate specialist.

Once a diagnosis has been made by a suitably qualified person, the sports massage therapist may often provide treatment which will benefit the client. For example, musculo-skeletal imbalances (*see* pp. 56–9) may often arise as a result of a traumatic injury – and these may be accurately assessed and treated by the sports massage therapist. For this reason, many sports massage therapists will often work in tandem with other sports-care specialists.

◆ Do you need to be ◆ fit and active in sport?

Sports massage is physically demanding and may involve long and continuous periods of strenuous work. As a therapist you need to have the strength and endurance to cope with extended periods of demanding physical activity. Your health and wellbeing are your most important assets, and overdoing it because of a lack of physical fitness can be detrimental to both you and your client.

As well as physical fitness, a therapist needs good mobility and flexibility to massage effectively. Good posture is essential, and guidelines on posture for massage are provided in Chapter 9.

While you don't need to be an active sports participant, knowing as much as you can about a client's activity will help you to understand how conditions may arise. It will also ensure you can provide sound advice that is relevant to your client's activity.

◆ Where is sports massage ◆ practised?

The sports massage therapist will be expected to carry out different forms of massage in various circumstances and surroundings: in a treatment room, at a sports event, on a sports field, at the trackside or in changing rooms either before, during or after a race or event. These venues may be noisy and crowded, unlike the tranquil environment often associated with other forms of massage that are aimed at relaxation. Furthermore, a therapist will often work among teams and large groups of people such as coaches, players, trainers and other sports therapists. Whatever the circumstances, it is essential to maintain a professional and confidential,

one-to-one client relationship. Information about setting up a treatment room for permanent or for temporary use is provided in Appendix 2, *The treatment room*.

◆ Do you need insurance ◆ to practise sports massage?

It is important to have *public liability* and *professional indemnity insurance* once you are qualified. Although it is unlikely that anyone will have reason to claim against you, it does provide your clients with the reassurance that you have adopted a professional approach – and that in the event of an accident while in your treatment area, they would be covered by adequate insurance.

For an annual premium of £60 at the time of writing, Independent Professional Therapists International (IPTI) provides all-risk insurance cover to the sum of £1 million (*see* p. 165 for contact details). This covers you for any damage or harm caused to your client while in your care. This might result from an accident, such as someone tripping over a badly placed doormat, or from negligence – for example, if harm were caused to your client by a particular technique you have applied. Both situations are very rare, but it's best to be covered.

The £1 million mentioned above is not a ceiling, and can be increased for an additional premium, which may be necessary if you are dealing with elite and highly paid athletes.

♦ What equipment does ♦ a sports therapist need?

To practise sports massage you will need a basic kit that includes the items detailed below.

Portable couch

If you intend working in sport, it is almost certain that you will have to travel to sports events, either with teams or individuals. It is therefore important to have a well-constructed, portable couch that folds in half, and a tough and durable carrying case to protect it from damage during transit. *See* Appendix 1 for further information on the massage couch.

Bath towels and couch cover

You will need at least two bath towels. One may be folded and rolled to support your client behind the knees in the supine position (lying on the back), and under the ankles in the prone position (lying on the front). The other towel may be used to cover your client for comfort and/or warmth. It is important to use bath towels, as smaller towels often prove inadequate for these purposes. A pillow or a third bath towel is also recommended for supporting your client's head when they are lying in the supine position.

Some form of towelling cover for the couch is essential and the best ones available on the market have an elasticated edge that holds the cover in place. If you are working in the field it is advisable to have a roll of tissue for additional covering for the couch (it should match the width of your couch), which you can replace between massage sessions. This is often necessary because you may be working with athletes who are muddy or, at the very least, perspiring.

Flannels

A supply of flannels is useful, particularly at sports events, for removing dirt and excess oil. Flannels are used with sports cologne (*see* below) for the removal of oil. They will become grubby quickly, so it is sensible to have a number in reserve.

Massage oil and sports cologne

There are various forms of *massage oil* available, and what you choose depends on your own preferences and those of your clients. The purest form of vegetable oil with little or no fragrance added is recommended to reduce the possibility of adverse skin reactions. Some essential oils may be added in very small quantities for general use, such as lavender and lemongrass, which are known to be effective muscle relaxants. However, if you are going to use essential oils in massage you should undertake appropriate training in aromatherapy – essential oils are contra-indicated in some conditions, such as pregnancy. *See* Appendix 3 for guidelines on using essential oils in sports massage.

Sports cologne is used for removing any excess oil at the end of a massage session. Although most of the oil is usually absorbed into the skin, clients like to be assured that it will not rub on to their clothes after the massage. You may also find, particularly at events with large numbers of participants, that it is impossible for the organisers to provide washing or showering facilities, either for the athletes or the sports massage therapists. In these situations, sports cologne is ideal for removing any dirt from your client and for cleaning your hands before massaging. Finally, when working at sports events, and particularly in pre-competition situations, you will probably find that many athletes prefer not to have the oil left on when competing – sports cologne is therefore ideal in these circumstances.

Talcum powder

Talcum powder is a widely used massage medium, although oil tends to be preferred. It is advisable, therefore, to have a small container of talcum powder with you for occasions when a client prefers this to massage oil. This may be the case in some competitions, such as aerobics, where the competitors are not allowed to appear with any type of oil on their skin.

♦ Guidelines on personal ♦ hygiene

As physical contact is the essence of sports massage, the appearance and personal hygiene of the sports massage therapist are of the utmost importance. Hair should always be clean and tied back when necessary to avoid contact with the client. Special attention should be given to your hands: nails must be kept short and the skin must be kept clean at all times. Always wash your hands between treatment sessions. If this is not possible when you are working in the field, cologne is a very effective substitute (*see* above).

Additional guidelines for the sports massage therapist are provided in Chapter 14, *Tips for success*.

PART TWO

The science of sports massage

Chapter 3

The principles of human anatomy and physiology

Knowledge and an understanding of the human body and how it functions is the starting point of sports massage theory. The more we understand about how the body functions, what may interrupt this functioning (such as trauma and injury), and what influence increased activity has on the systems that combine to make it function, the more the sports massage therapist can use their skills and knowledge to advise their clients. This chapter looks at the various systems that make up the body, and how parts and movements of the body are described. The information in this chapter is intended only as a foundation and further study is encouraged (*see* p. 164 *Recommended reading*).

First, a few definitions:

♦ *Anatomy* is the study of the structure of the human body and its component parts.
♦ *Physiology* is the study of how the body and its systems function.

♦ The body systems ♦

There are 10 major systems that function within the human body.

The skeletal system

The skeletal system is the framework of the body, and comprises approximately 206 bones and their associated cartilages. The bones of the head, neck and trunk contribute to the *axial skeleton;* those of the limbs form the *appendicular skeleton.*

The muscular system

This is responsible for moving bones at joints and consists of skeletal muscle in association with tendons and ligaments. Two other muscle tissues are also described: cardiac muscle, aptly named, as it is found only in the heart; and smooth muscle, which is widely distributed in the walls of many hollow tubes in the body (e.g. the gut and blood vessels).

The cardiovascular (circulatory) system

This is responsible for transporting the blood around, so that cells throughout the body can be supplied with oxygen and nutrients and their waste products removed. The cardiovascular system includes the heart and blood vessels (principally arteries, arterioles, capillaries, venules and veins), and is closely related to the *lymphatic* system. This consists of blindly-ending lymphatic vessels, and is concerned with removing excess tissue fluid and returning it to the blood system via the great veins in the neck.

The respiratory system

The respiratory system comprises the lungs and their associated airways (e.g. the nasal cavity, larynx and trachea). It is concerned with allowing oxygen and carbon dioxide to be exchanged between the blood and the air.

The digestive system

This system is concerned with the ingestion of food, the absorption of the products of digestion, and the excretion of indigestible waste products. It extends from the mouth to the anus and includes the oral cavity, pharynx, oesophagus, stomach, small and large intestines and various associated glands – notably the liver, pancreas and salivary glands.

The nervous system

Comprises the brain and spinal cord (which together form the central nervous system), as well as peripheral autonomic nerves (which together constitute the peripheral nervous system). The nervous system enables the body to adapt to changes in either the external or the internal environment.

The excretory (urinary) system

Comprises the kidneys, ureters, bladder and urethra. It is concerned with producing, transporting, storing and excreting urine. (*Note*: Other systems, including the digestive, respiratory and the integumentary systems, also remove waste products.)

The endocrine (hormonal) system

Consists of the endocrine glands – including the pituitary, adrenal, thyroid, parathyroid, pineal, testes and ovaries, and the pancreatic islets of Langerhans – which secrete hormones directly into the bloodstream. These hormones affect a wide range of body functions. For example, the pituitary gland secretes hormones affecting skeletal growth, the development of the sex glands and the functioning of other endocrine glands; and the adrenal glands produce adrenaline and noradrenaline.

The integumentary system

This comprises of the skin and its 'appendages' (hairs, sweat glands, sebaceous glands and nails).

The reproductive system

Comprises all the sexual organs concerned with reproduction.

In sports massage the two most important body systems are the *skeletal system* and the *muscular system* (also described collectively as the *musculo-skeletal system*). These will be covered in detail in this chapter. Four of the other systems – the cardiovascular, respiratory, digestive and nervous – also play a role in the theory and practice of sports massage and are discussed briefly.

♦ Anatomical terminology ♦

In order to understand and communicate the parts and movements of the body to other people, you need to know the terms used to describe them. The key terms are considered below in three categories: *axes and planes of the body, positions of the body*, and *movements of the body*.

Axes and planes of the body

There are four planes and associated axes of the body, which are illustrated in Figure 3.1.

♦ The *saggital plane* is any vertical longitudinal plane that is parallel to the median plane.
♦ The *frontal (coronal) plane* is the vertical plane that lies at right angles to both the median and the frontal planes and divides the body into front and back halves.
♦ The *transverse (horizontal) plane* is the plane that passes at right angles to both the median and the frontal planes and divides the body into upper and lower parts.

Note: The *median (midsaggital) plane* – not shown in Figure 3.1, is sometimes referred to. This is a vertical longitudinal plane that divides the body into right and left halves.

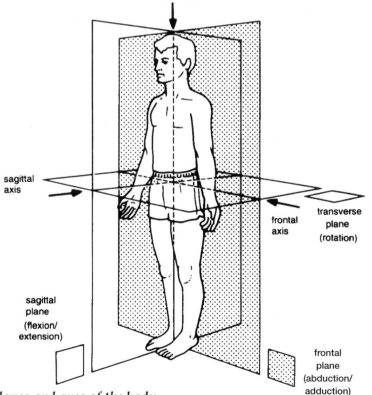

Figure 3.1 The planes and axes of the body

Positions of the body

The anatomical terms for describing positions of parts of the body are listed below and illustrated in Figure 3.2.

♦ *Medial* – nearer to the median plane (*see* above).
♦ *Lateral* – further from the median plane (*see* above).
♦ *Proximal* – nearer to the point of attachment of a limb to the trunk.
♦ *Distal* – further from the point of attachment of a limb to the trunk.
♦ *Anterior (ventral)* – towards the front of the body.
♦ *Posterior (dorsal)* – towards the back of the body.
♦ *Inferior* – closer to the feet.
♦ *Superior* – closer to the head.

Additionally, the following two terms are important to the sports massage therapist, as they describe the two main positions of the client during sports massage:

♦ *Supine* – describes the position of a body lying horizontal and face up.
♦ *Prone* describes the position of a body lying horizontal and face down.

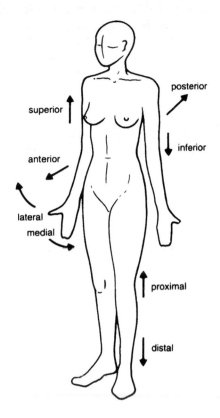

Figure 3.2 Anatomical terms for describing the positions of parts of the body

Movements of the body

The anatomical terms for describing movements of the body are listed below and illustrated in Figure 3.3 overleaf.

♦ *Flexion* – a reduction in the angle between bones at a joint, i.e. bending the joint.
♦ *Extension* – an increase in the angle between bones at a joint, i.e. straightening the joint.
♦ *Abduction* – movement of a limb away from the median plane (*see* above).
♦ *Adduction* – movement of a limb towards the median plane (*see* above).

♦ *Circumduction* – a circular limb movement which combines in sequence flexion, extension, abduction, and adduction.
♦ *Rotation* – movement of a limb around its long axis. *Medial rotation* turns the anterior surface medially, and *lateral rotation* turns it laterally.
♦ *Dorsiflexion* – movement of the foot to point the toes upwards.
♦ *Plantarflexion* – movement of the foot to point the toes downwards.
♦ *Protraction* of the scapula draws the shoulder girdle forwards around the chest wall.

13

- *Retraction* of the scapula draws the shoulder girdle backwards around the chest wall, so that the shoulders are 'braced' as in a military stance.
- *Elevation* of the shoulder girdle lifts the scapula upwards, as in shrugging the shoulders.
- *Depression* of the shoulder girdle lifts the scapula downwards so as to lower the shoulders.
- *Supination* – a rotary movement of the forearm so that the palm faces upwards.

- *Pronation* – a rotary movement of the forearm so the palm faces downwards. (*Note:* The terms 'pronation' and 'supination' are sometimes also applied to complex movements of the foot – a 'pronated' foot is a flat foot.)
- *Inversion* – turning the sole of the foot inwards.
- *Eversion* – turning the sole of the foot outwards.
- *Lateral flexion* of the trunk bends it in the frontal plane (*see* above).

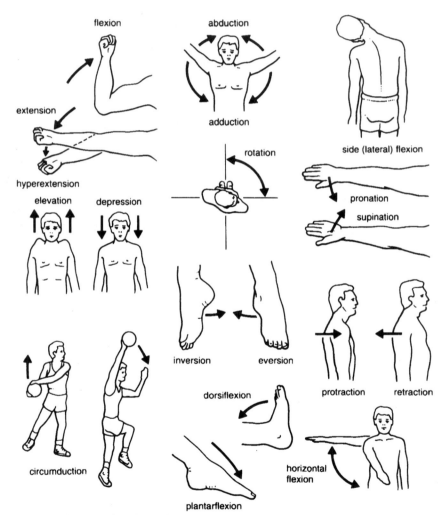

Figure 3.3 Anatomical terms for describing movements of parts of the body

♦ The skeletal system ♦

The skeletal system is made up of bones and cartilage, and is one of the most important of the body systems in the application of sports massage. This is because the therapist identifies the position of other body structures in relation to bony prominences that form 'landmarks' – *see* Chapter 8 on surface anatomy and palpation.

The sports massage therapist also needs to understand joint range of motion (where two bones meet) and the locations of muscle attachments. All of these enhance an understanding of physical activity and movement, and in turn help with the processes of identification and assessment.

The functions and component parts of the skeletal system, together with conditions which may affect it, are discussed below. Ligaments are included in this discussion, because although they are classified as 'soft tissue', they attach bone to bone and provide stability to joints by limiting movement beyond a certain range. (Tendons form part of muscles, and provide points of attachment to other structures – usually bone. As such, they are discussed on p. 22, under *The muscular system*.)

Functions of the skeletal system

Support
Bones and cartilage form the majority of rigid materials in the body. (Enamel and dentine of the teeth are also rigid, but are not bone.) The numerous bones of the skeleton provide a framework for the body, and a means of attachment for muscles and other soft tissues of the body.

Protection
The skeletal structures protect some of the vital tissues and organs of the body. For example, the skull protects the brain, the vertebrae protect the spinal cord, and the thoracic cage protects the heart and lungs.

Movement
Bones act as *levers* during movement (*see* also p. 22, *The muscular system*) and provide rigid structures to which muscles attach. The joints allow movement between bones, and these movements are directly related to the type of joint and range of motion. Movement of the skeletal system is discussed in more detail in the section on joints later in this chapter (*see* pp. 17–18).

Storage
Some bones contain red bone marrow that produces red blood cells, white cells, and *platelets* or *thrombocytes* – small, non-nuclear structures containing cytoplasm, which repair slightly damaged vessels and are essential to initiating the clotting process. Minerals, especially calcium and phosphorous, are also stored in bones and can be distributed to other parts of the body.

Bone structure and growth

Bone is composed of approximately 25 per cent water, 45 per cent mineral (mainly calcium phosphate), and 30 per cent organic matter (mainly collagen). The organic matter consists of fibrous material that gives bones their toughness and resilience; the minerals in the bones give them rigidity and hardness.

The general structure of a bone is as follows.

♦ *Compact bone* forms the external layer of a bone and is designed to withstand considerable stress. It forms the tubular shaft of long bones, a structure that gives them the ability to combine maximum strength with minimum weight.

♦ *Haversian canals* are microscopic units of compact bone structure consisting of a central Haversian system (*see* below).

♦ *The Haversian system* contains blood and lymphatic vessels surrounded by numerous layers or 'lamellae' of bone matrix.

♦ *Osteocytes* are mature bone cells within the matrix that are responsible for its maintenance.

♦ *Osteoblasts* are bone-forming cells, which secrete the matrix referred to above. When they have finished doing so they become osteocytes (*see* above).

♦ *Cancellous* (or spongy) bone, found underneath the compact bone, is a lattice-like network of thin bone plates with irregular spaces filled with red bone marrow.

♦ *Periosteum* is a fibrous surface membrane on the bone and is important for the bone's growth, blood supply and muscle attachments.

The process by which bone is formed is known as *ossification*. Some bones, such as the flat bones of the skull, are formed directly from ordinary connective tissue, a process called *intramembranous ossification*. Other bones (notably all the long bones of the limbs), are formed initially as mini-cartilage models. During the growth periods, the cartilage is eroded and replaced by bone. This process is called *endochondral ossification*.

The skeleton of a human embryo is made up of *hyaline cartilage* (*see* p. 17) and connective tissue membrane. Ossification starts at about the sixth week of embryonic life and continues through puberty into adulthood. Full development is complete by about the age of 25. In a typical long bone (e.g. the humerus), ossification starts before birth in the shaft (*diaphysis*) by a formation of a primary centre of ossification. Secondary centres of ossification appear after birth at the ends of the long bone – at the *epiphyses*. Growth plates of cartilage remain between the two and promote the growth in the length of the long bone. The bone grows in width because of the activity of its periosteum. Growth is over when the growth plate 'closes', although bone continues to adapt its structure throughout life according to the various forces and stresses imposed upon it.

When bones are fractured they are initially repaired by a material called *callus*, which is produced rapidly to stabilise the bone defect. Callus is eventually completely replaced by compact bone.

Types of bone

There are five types of bone based on differences in their shape.

♦ *Long bones* are found in the limbs and are the strongest bones in the body. An example is the thigh bone (femur).

♦ *Short bones* are found in the wrist and the foot – for example, the scaphoid in the hand.

♦ *Flat bones* include the shoulder blades (scapulae) and those found in the skull, for example the frontal bone.

♦ *Sesamoid bones* are small, seed-shaped bones embedded in the substance of tendons – for example, the patella in the quadriceps tendon.

♦ *Irregular bones* include the vertebrae, hipbones, and many facial bones.

Joints

A joint, or *articulation*, is formed where two or more bones meet. Joints are divided according to their mobility into the following three categories:

♦ *Fixed fibrous joints* (or *synarthroses*) do not allow movement and have tough fibrous tissues holding the bones together. The bones in the skull are an example.
♦ *Slightly movable joints* (or *amphiarthroses*) allow small movements. They are held together by ligaments (*see* below) and separated by pads of fibrocartilage. An example is the pelvic bone joint of the symphysis pubis.
♦ *Freely movable joints* (or *diarthroses*) are synovial joints (*see* below) and are the main type of joints found in the human body. They are further categorised into: ball-and-socket joints (e.g. hip joint); hinge joints (e.g. knee and elbow joints); pivot joints (e.g. radius and ulna joints); plane joints (e.g. acromioclavicular joint).

Range of motion (ROM) is the amount of movement in a joint between its two extreme points. The limiting factors are either the mechanics of the joint itself, or the muscle and other soft tissue which act upon it. As detailed above, there are various types of joints and each type is designed to allow a certain range of movement. Range of motion is discussed further in Chapter 11.

Joint structures and functions

All joint structures are made up of some of the components detailed below, each of which plays an important part in the function and stability of a joint. As sports massage is mainly concerned with movement, the component parts of a synovial joint are examined below.

Synovial joints
The basic structure of a synovial joint includes a fibrous capsule and ligaments that link the bones. The stability of these joints is determined by the shape of the joint surfaces and their surrounding ligaments and muscles. For example, the strength of the knee is determined by two cruciate and two collateral ligaments, while one of the hardest joints to dislocate, the hip, is formed with the head of the femur fitting neatly into the socket (*acetabulum*) in the pelvis.

Cartilage
Articular (*hyaline*) cartilage covers and protects the ends of the bones where they meet to form a joint, to allow freedom of movement. It is a very smooth material that does not repair itself easily when damaged, but gives flexibility and support, and reduces friction. *Fibrocartilage* contains many bundles of collagenous fibres and gives strength and rigidity to the menisci in the knee (often referred to as cartilage), intervertebral discs in the spine and the pubic symphysis pubis (where two bony surfaces in the lower part of the pelvis meet).

Elastic cartilage combines strength and elasticity for structures such as the epiglottis in the larynx and external part of the ear.

Ligaments
Ligaments are tough, fibrous bands of soft tissue that connect bones and help stabilise joints. One of the strongest ligaments in the body is that situated at the front of the hip capsule, preventing excessive backward movement of the legs. Ligaments, although stronger than muscle tissue, have less blood supply and therefore take longer to repair when damaged. While these strong fibrous bands stabilise a joint by preventing excessive movement, if they are stretched or torn through injury they do not necessarily return to their former length, which may result in reduced stability and excessive mobility of the affected joint.

Synovial membrane

Synovial membrane lines the parts of the joint cavity that are not covered by articular cartilage (*see* above), and covers the tendons and ligaments that pass through it. The membrane produces synovial fluid, which lubricates the joint and nourishes its tissues.

Bursa

A bursa is a small, fluid-filled sac which is formed in connective tissue and lined by a synovial membrane. It is situated between moving parts, often between tendon and bone, to prevent rubbing.

Identification of bones

The bones of the human body are divided into the *axial* skeleton, comprising the skull, ribs, sternum and vertebral column; and the *appendicular* skeleton, comprising the upper and lower limbs and the girdles (shoulder and pelvic) that connect the limbs to the *axial* skeleton. Figure 3.4 (*see* p. 19) shows the human skeleton, and may be cross-referenced to Table 3.1 opposite.

The bones that make up the human body are listed in Table 3.1. You may find that some anatomy and physiology books list further bones – for example, the hyoid and auditory ossicles – or count the sacrum and coccyx as one bone, since their constituent skeletal elements are fused.

Table 3.1 The bones of the human body

Axial skeleton	
Skull	
Cranium	8 bones
Face	14 bones
Vertebral column	
Cervical	7 bones
Thoracic	12 bones
Lumbar	5 bones
Sacrum	5 (fused) bones
Coccyx	4 (fused) bones
Thorax	
Sternum	1 bone
Ribs	24 bones
Appendicular skeleton	
Pectoral (shoulder) girdle	
Clavicle	2 bones
Scapula	2 bones
Upper limb	
Humerus	2 bones
Ulna	2 bones
Radius	2 bones
Carpals	16 bones
Metacarpals	10 bones
Phalanges	28 bones
Pelvic (hip) girdle	
Coxal pelvic or hipbone	2 bones
Lower limbs	
Femur	2 bones
Fibula	2 bones
Tibia	2 bones
Patella	2 bones
Tarsals	14 bones
Metatarsals	10 bones
Phalanges	28 bones

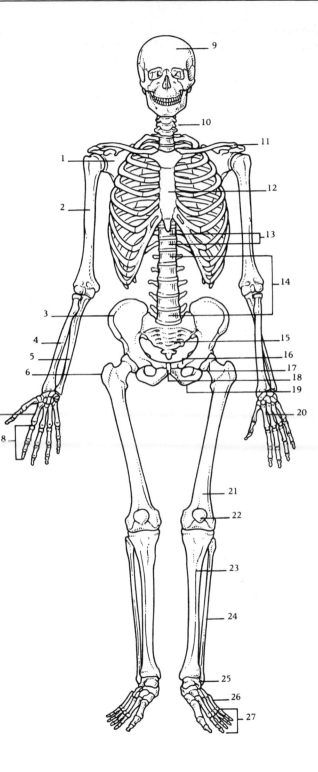

1 scapula (shoulder blade)
2 humerus
3 ilium (hipbone)
4 radius
5 ulna
6 (greater trochanter)
7 metacarpals (palm facing forwards)
8 phalanges (palm facing forwards)
9 skull
10 cervical vertebrae
11 clavicle (collar bone)
12 sternum (breastbone)
13 eleventh and twelfth thoracic vertebrae
14 lumbar vertebrae
15 sacrum
16 pubis
17 hip joint
18 (symphysis pubis)
19 (ischium)
20 carpus (palm facing backwards)
21 femur (thigh bone)
22 patella (knee cap)
23 tibia
24 fibula
25 tarsus
26 metatarsals
27 phalanges

Figure 3.4 The human skeleton

Differences in female and male skeletons

Female and male skeletons differ in the form of the pelvis, with the female being wider and flatter to facilitate childbirth. This also means the angle of the femur from the hip to the knee tends to be greater. (This is often known as a 'Q' angle and may have an important influence on knee problems, particularly for endurance athletes such as marathon runners.) Males, on the other hand, are generally taller with greater muscle bulk, so the bones of the male skeleton are heavier and the markings left on them where tendons attach are more prominent.

The spine

The spine comprises a series of bones forming a flexible, strong column that allows movement and at the same time affords protection to the spinal cord. The structure of each vertebra, along with the intervetebral discs situated between each pair of bones, allows considerable mobility including flexion, extension, lateral flexion and rotation – while still maintaining the centre support for the entire body. The intervertebral discs are also believed by some authorities to act as shock absorbers against impact. Figure 3.5

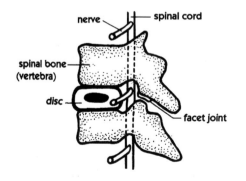

Figure 3.5 The structure of a spinal segment

shows the structure of a spinal segment. The spine is extremely resilient, but if it is damaged in any way the consequences are often serious because the spinal cord, which carries nerve impulses to and from the brain, may be immediately affected.

Conditions affecting the skeleton

The process of ageing has two main effects on bone structure. First, bones begin to lose calcium; this is one of the factors contributing to osteoporosis (*see* below). Loss of calcium is more common in women and can begin from the age of 30. The process accelerates around the ages of 40 to 45 as oestrogen levels decrease. In men, calcium loss tends not to begin until after the age of 60 (*see* also Chapter 4 on the effects of exercise on the human body). Second, less protein is produced as we age, which alters the make-up of bone and sometimes creates brittle bones. The following is a list of conditions which may affect the skeleton.

♦ *Ankylosis* – stiffness or fixation of a joint.
♦ *Bursitis* – inflammation of the bursa (*see* p. 18).
♦ *Dislocation* – where at least two articulating surfaces have become separated. Usually involves damage to other tissues, such as the ligaments and the joint capsule.
♦ *Fracture* – a break in a bone. The main types are defined below:
    Simple fracture: a bone is broken and causes no serious damage to surrounding soft tissue.
    Complicated fracture: a bone is broken and causes damage to surrounding soft tissue.
    Compound fracture: a bone is broken and one or both ends protrude through the skin.
    Comminuted fracture: a bone is broken in a number of places.

Impact fracture: a bone is broken and one end is driven into the other.

Greenstick fracture: an incomplete fracture (of a long bone) as seen in young children.

♦ *Osteoarthritis* – a disease caused by the degeneration of cartilage. This gradually gets eroded so that the underlying bone is exposed.
♦ *Osteitis* – inflammation of bone.
♦ *Osteomyelitis* – infection of bone.
♦ *Osteoporosis* – a disease caused by the loss of calcium from the bones (*see* also above). The bones become brittle and fracture more easily. The disease is prevalent in post-menopausal women. Women who have trained intensively for a long period of time and start menopause prematurely are also susceptible.
♦ *Osteosarcoma* – a malignant tumour growing from a bone that particularly affects young people.
♦ *Excessive spinal curvature* – there are three types, listed below and illustrated in Figure 3.6. These conditions may be caused, or exaggerated, by: hereditary (congenital) factors; trauma resulting from accident or injury; environmental factors (leading to bad posture); diseases affecting either the bones of the spine or the structures supporting it.

Kyphosis: the outward curvature of the thoracic region of the spine is exaggerated.

Lordosis: the inward curvature of the lumbar region of the spine is exaggerated.

Scoliosis: the lateral curvature of any section of the spine is exaggerated.

♦ *Sprains* – result from the stretching or tearing of ligaments within a joint.
♦ *Subluxation* – partial dislocation where the articulating surfaces have not become completely separated.
♦ *Synovitis* – the inflammation of synovial membrane (*see* p. 18).

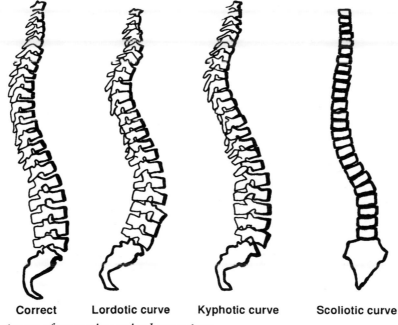

Correct   **Lordotic curve**   **Kyphotic curve**   **Scoliotic curve**

Figure 3.6 The three types of excessive spinal curvature

◆ The muscular system ◆

Muscles of the body are responsible for maintaining posture and bringing about movement. They combine with the skeletal system to form a complex and finely balanced system of levers. Muscles are capable of contraction, but not active extension – which can only be achieved by a muscle relaxing while the opposing muscle contracts. Muscles can maintain a state of partial contraction known as *muscle tone,* so they must be stretched to maintain body suppleness, condition and balance within the musculo-skeletal system. This is important for anyone who exercises, and is the most important system for the sports massage therapist to understand since it has the greatest influence in achieving physical activity. The muscles of the human body are shown in Figure 3.8(a) and (b) on pp. 27–8.

Functions of the muscular system

Motion
The main framework of the body is covered by muscle, whose function is to permit movement. To understand how the muscles and skeleton combine to produce movement involves studying the basic mechanics of movement. To produce movement, the musculo-skeletal system adopts the principle of *leverage;* this dictates that to move or lift a load against another force, it is easier to use levers. When applying this principle to the human body, movement is a combination of the following:

◆ the *lever,* which is nearly always the bone;
◆ the *fulcrum,* the pivot point of the lever, which is usually the joint;
◆ *muscle force* that draws the opposite ends of the muscles together;

◆ *resistive force* that acts against the muscle force and is generated by a factor external to the body (e.g. gravity or friction);
◆ *torque* that determines the degree to which the forces rotate the lever about the fulcrum.

Types of body movements and their anatomical descriptions are discussed on pp. 13–14.

Heat production
Muscle contractions produce heat; as much as 70 per cent of body heat is energy produced in muscle tissue. Blood plays an essential role in controlling heat production and body temperature during exercise. When the body is overheating, blood takes heat from the body core and working muscles and redirects it to the skin. When the internal heat of the body reaches too low a level, thermoreceptors in the skin relay a message to the brain, in response to which the skeletal muscles contract and relax in an involuntary manner (shivering) – increasing muscle activity to generate heat.

Muscles are also responsive to external heat: cold air increases muscle tone, and hot conditions have a relaxing effect on muscles.

Maintenance of posture
As well as enabling movement, muscles also maintain *posture* and *body position.* Sensory receptors in the muscles monitor the tension and length of the muscles, and provide the nervous system with crucial information about the position of the body parts to enable posture to be maintained. The tension or tone produced as a result of muscle contractions between various opposing groups of muscle helps us to maintain posture, even when we are asleep.

Properties of muscle

Muscle tissue has four main properties:

♦ *Excitability* – the ability to respond to stimuli.
♦ *Contractability* – the ability to contract.
♦ *Extensibility* – the ability to be stretched without tearing.
♦ *Elasticity* – the ability to return to its normal shape after stretching.

Types of Muscle

Skeletal muscle

As the name suggests, skeletal muscles are usually attached to bones and move parts of the skeleton. They are a form of *striated* muscle, because the bundles of muscle fibres have a striped appearance when viewed under a microscope. Skeletal muscle is *voluntary* muscle tissue, i.e. is under our conscious control.

The individual muscle fibres within a skeletal muscle are giant elongated cells, surrounded by a delicate connective tissue called *endomysium* and grouped together into bundles called *fascicles*. These in turn are surrounded by further connective tissue called *perimysium*. Finally, all the fascicles are collected together in a further connective tissue wrapping that surrounds the muscle as a whole and is known as the *epimysium*. Each fibre has its contractile filaments (called *actin* and *myosin* filaments) grouped into bundles within the cell. When the muscle contracts, its actin and myosin filaments slide across each other to shorten the length of the fibre. This is part of what is known as the '*sliding filament theory*' (*see* also p. 128). Figure 3.7 illustrates the structure of skeletal muscle.

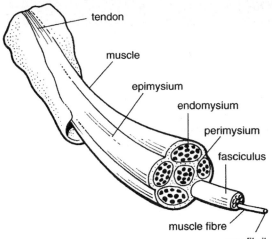

Figure 3.7 The structure of skeletal muscle

Fascia

This is a general term for any sheet of connective tissue in the body. Among the most important ones in sports therapy are the *superficial* and *deep fascias of the limbs*, although these and other fascias are found in other regions as well. The former is a loose connective tissue that links the skin to the underlying structures and allows it to move over them. It is where much tissue fluid accumulates (e.g. in swollen ankles) and where infections are both fought and spread. The deep fascia is a denser and tougher connective tissue that lies beneath the superficial fascia and surrounds limb muscles like a stocking. It is also attached to the limb bones and thus divides groups of muscles into compartments. These compartments are particularly significant in the leg, where 'compartment syndromes' can result from muscle swellings within the deep fascial restraints that increase compartmental pressure.

Tendons

Tendons are pieces of dense connective tissue that link muscles to bone. Although tendons are more elastic than ligaments, and their recoil economises on muscular effort, they have a far greater tensile strength than muscle. They allow a muscle to attach to a very precise point on a bone and thus contribute greatly to the precision of limb movements – particularly those of the hand. Tendons allow muscles to pull through narrow spaces like the carpal tunnel in the wrist, and to pull around corners (like the malleoli of the ankle). Many have associated synovial sheaths that act like the outer covering of a break cable, allowing the tendons to move freely as their muscles contract. However, these can get damaged from repetitive motion (e.g. at the wrist in tennis players). Some tendons, notably the Achilles, have a 'false' or non-synovial sheath that can get inflamed and lead to heel pain – often prevalent in endurance runners, for example. Tendons generally attach to bone with bits of fibrocartilage that protect them as they bend with joint movements. However, the attachment points are frequently injured in sport, causing such complaints as tennis elbow, or golfer's elbow. Like ligaments, tendons have a relatively poor blood supply and this adds to the difficulty of repair. They also have relatively few cells, so making new tendon substance is difficult in adults. The point where a tendon links to its muscle is called the myotendinous junction and this is where most muscle strains or pulls occur.

Types of skeletal muscle fibre

Skeletal muscle fibres can be classed as *slow twitch (type I)* or *fast twitch (types IIA and IIB)*. Slow-twitch (ST) fibres are the smaller and produce less overall force. They play a major role in endurance activities such as marathons, triathlons and cycle tours, for they are relatively resistant to fatigue. They are rich in mitochondria, which in turn contain enzymes involved in aerobic respiration, and they have a rich blood capillary supply. Fast-twitch (FT) fibres – type IIB – are larger, fatigue easily and predominate in explosive activities such as sprinting and weightlifting. They have fewer mitochondria than type I fibres, but are well endowed with the necessary enzymes for anaerobic respiration and have good stores of glycogen. They react to athletic training by 'hypertrophy' (or cell enlargement), and thus anabolic steroids are specifically aimed at enhancing their activity. In contrast, type I fibres change little in size with exercise.

Type IIA fibres have characteristics intermediate between those of types I and IIB fibres. There seem to be no muscles in man that are composed exclusively of just one muscle type; the exact proportion of fibre types in different muscles varies between individuals and is genetically determined. Hence an athletics sprint coach will be looking for athletes with many fast-twitch fibres, and a long-distance coach will be looking for someone with a lot of type I fibres. Although it is still a debated point, it seems unlikely that you can greatly alter the proportion of fibre types by training. Training increases fibre size and it can increase muscle blood supply, but it probably does not influence the proportion of types.

Muscle fibre recruitment

During low-intensity work (e.g. walking) the body is working well below its maximal capacity and only ST muscle fibres are working. As muscle intensity increases and the exercise becomes more anaerobic, FT fibres are activated. Whatever the intensity or fibre recruitment, only a small number of fibres are used at any one time to prevent damage and injury to the tissue. If all fibres were recruited at the same time, the generated force may damage the muscle. However, as healthy tendons have far greater strength than muscle tissue, they are much less likely to be affected. (*See* Chapter 4, pp. 46–7 for further discussion on muscle fibres.)

Cardiac muscle

Cardiac muscle forms the bulk of the heart and is called the *myocardium*. The thickness of cardiac muscle varies throughout the heart walls; the left ventricle (or chamber) has the thickest walls, as blood has to be pumped from it to the entire body with the exception of the lungs. Like skeletal muscle, increases in demand caused by intense exercise will increase the size of the muscle.

A cardiac muscle fibre consists of many individual cells joined end to end, and is an involuntary muscle that contracts rhythmically at a rate determined by a *pacemaker*. Thus heart rate cannot be controlled by the conscious will. The pacemaker consists of modified cardiac muscle fibres that are controlled by autonomic nerves. The signal for contraction spreads from one cell to another within each fibre via special junctional regions called '*intercalated discs*'. Cardiac muscle is thus very different from skeletal muscle (*see* p. 23), even though both are classed as being made up of striated fibres. It does not fatigue readily unless the rate of contractions (the *heart rate*) is increased for a prolonged period without sufficient rest. The resting heart rate averages 70 beats (contractions) per minute.

Smooth muscle

Smooth muscle typically occurs in sheets or layers in the walls of a great number of hollow tubes in the body – e.g. blood vessels and the gut. It allows them either to change their calibre (blood vessels) or to propel material along the lumen (gut). It is an involuntary muscle, which, because of its function, is able to contract over many hours without fatigue.

How do muscles contract?

In order for a muscle to contract, it needs large amounts of energy. A 'message' (nerve impulse) is also required from the brain to initiate action. The body's ability to create energy relies on a compound called *adenosine triphosphate* (*ATP*), which is made in the muscle cells. When exercise begins, *creatine phosphate*, a substance stored in the muscle, combines with *adenosine diphosphate* (*ADP*) and forms ATP for energy production. After about the first 10 seconds of exercise, stores of ATP are depleted and the muscle will convert ATP from carbohydrate that is stored in the form of glycogen. The methods adopted to generate ATP after these initial stages rely on three forms of energy production, which are discussed in detail in Chapter 4, (*see* pp. 44–6) Once the energy has been utilised, waste products (such as lactic acid) are created; these are removed from muscle tissue to prevent build-up.

Each muscle fibre is innervated by a nerve called a *motor neuron*. A single motor neuron supplies a number of muscle fibres and collectively they are known as a *motor unit*. Communication between the nervous and muscular systems occurs at the neuromuscular junction or *motor end plate*. For a muscle fibre to 'fire', a nerve impulse arrives at the nerve's endings, which are located very close to the *sarcolemma* (the cell membrane of a muscle fibre). The gap between the nerve's endings and the muscle fibre must be bridged for the nerve impulse to activate the muscle – this is achieved indirectly by the secretion of a neurotransmitter called *acetylcholine* (*ACh*). (Further information on motor nerve impulses is included in the section on the nervous system later in this chapter.) Depending on the particular muscle, a single motor neuron can innervate from one to several hundred muscle fibres.

The speed at which a muscle contracts and how long the contraction is sustained is partly determined by how quickly the blood flow brings nourishment and oxygen to the muscle and removes the deoxygenated blood and waste products. This, in turn, is directly affected by the type of exercise undertaken and whether oxygen is used, as in aerobic exercise, or not, as in anaerobic exercise. As oxygen is needed to remove waste products from the muscle, anaerobic exercise – which accumulates waste material more rapidly – is only suitable for short periods of exercise – such as sprinting. Chapter 4 discusses these energy systems and the relevance for the different exercise intensities in detail.

Group action of muscles

Virtually all body movements involve the action of more than one muscle. The muscle primarily responsible for bringing about a movement is called the *agonist* or prime mover. At the same time as the agonist contracts, the opposing muscle, called the *antagonist*, relaxes, to allow the prime mover to move a joint in the desired range. For example, when the biceps brachii muscle contracts to flex (bend) the elbow, it is acting

as the agonist. However, the muscle resisting this movement is the triceps brachii muscle – the antagonist. It is important to note that antagonists can also contract at the same time as agonists, to control or slow down a movement. In the thigh, for example, the hamstrings do this for the quadriceps muscle during sprinting to stop the knee joint being damaged by forceful extension.

Identification of muscles

Figures 3.8(a) and 3.8(b) show the muscles of the human body – front and rear view respectively. These may be cross-referred to Tables 3.2 to 3.9 (pp. 29–39), which identify the muscles of the body in groups according to the body part they move: neck; shoulder girdle; shoulder joint; forearm and wrist; trunk; hip; knee; ankle and foot. The type of movement and the location of each muscle are also included.

Superficial Muscles

Deep Muscles

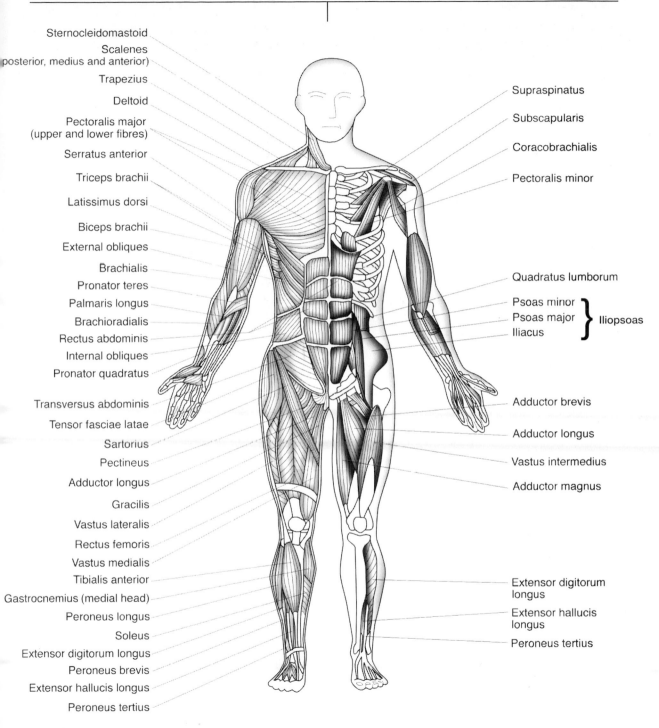

Sternocleidomastoid
Scalenes
(posterior, medius and anterior)
Trapezius
Deltoid
Pectoralis major
(upper and lower fibres)
Serratus anterior
Triceps brachii
Latissimus dorsi
Biceps brachii
External obliques
Brachialis
Pronator teres
Palmaris longus
Brachioradialis
Rectus abdominis
Internal obliques
Pronator quadratus
Transversus abdominis
Tensor fasciae latae
Sartorius
Pectineus
Adductor longus
Gracilis
Vastus lateralis
Rectus femoris
Vastus medialis
Tibialis anterior
Gastrocnemius (medial head)
Peroneus longus
Soleus
Extensor digitorum longus
Peroneus brevis
Extensor hallucis longus
Peroneus tertius

Supraspinatus
Subscapularis
Coracobrachialis
Pectoralis minor
Quadratus lumborum
Psoas minor
Psoas major   } Iliopsoas
Iliacus
Adductor brevis
Adductor longus
Vastus intermedius
Adductor magnus
Extensor digitorum longus
Extensor hallucis longus
Peroneus tertius

Figure 3.8(a) Muscles of the human body (front view)

Superficial Muscles

Deep Muscles

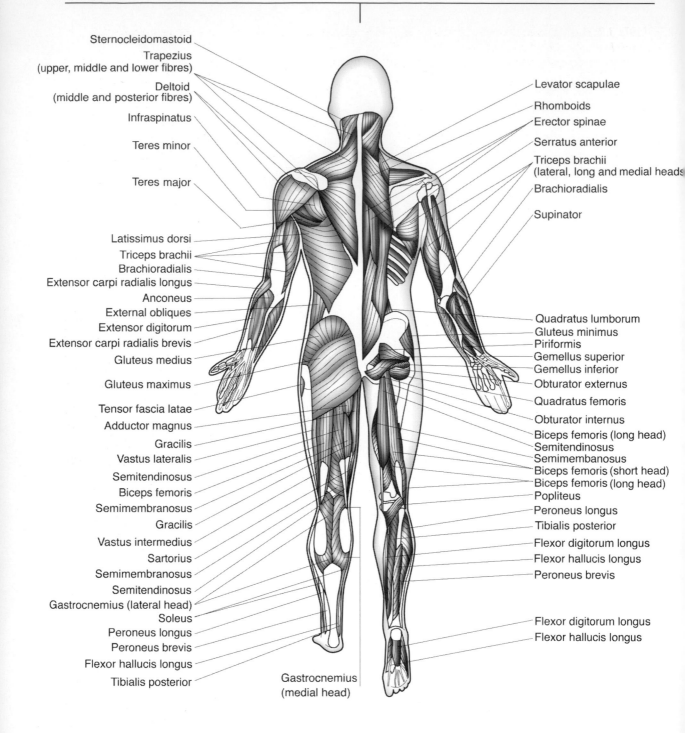

Sternocleidomastoid
Trapezius
(upper, middle and lower fibres)
Deltoid
(middle and posterior fibres)
Infraspinatus
Teres minor
Teres major
Latissimus dorsi
Triceps brachii
Brachioradialis
Extensor carpi radialis longus
Anconeus
External obliques
Extensor digitorum
Extensor carpi radialis brevis
Gluteus medius
Gluteus maximus
Tensor fascia latae
Adductor magnus
Gracilis
Vastus lateralis
Semitendinosus
Biceps femoris
Semimembranosus
Gracilis
Vastus intermedius
Sartorius
Semimembranosus
Semitendinosus
Gastrocnemius (lateral head)
Soleus
Peroneus longus
Peroneus brevis
Flexor hallucis longus
Tibialis posterior

Levator scapulae
Rhomboids
Erector spinae
Serratus anterior
Triceps brachii
(lateral, long and medial heads)
Brachioradialis
Supinator
Quadratus lumborum
Gluteus minimus
Piriformis
Gemellus superior
Gemellus inferior
Obturator externus
Quadratus femoris
Obturator internus
Biceps femoris (long head)
Semitendinosus
Semimembanosus
Biceps femoris (short head)
Biceps femoris (long head)
Popliteus
Peroneus longus
Tibialis posterior
Flexor digitorum longus
Flexor hallucis longus
Peroneus brevis
Flexor digitorum longus
Flexor hallucis longus

Gastrocnemius
(medial head)

Figure 3.8(b) Muscles of the human body (back view)

28

Table 3.2 Muscles that move the shoulder girdle (attach to shoulder girdle – scapula and/or clavicle and axial skeleton)

Muscle	Actions	Origins	Insertions
Levator scapulae	Raises (elevates scapula	Transverse processes of upper four cervical vertebrae	Superior medial border of scapula
Trapezius	*Upper fibres:* elevate scapula and clavicle; extend head *Middle fibres:* elevate, upwardly rotate and adduct scapula *Lower fibres:* depress, adduct and upwardly rotate scapula *Upper and lower:* together rotate scapula – important when arm is elevated	*Upper fibres:* base of skull, occipital protuberance, posterior ligaments of neck *Middle fibres:* spinous processes of seventh cervical vertebrae (C7) and upper three thoracic vertebrae (T1–3) *Lower fibres:* spinous process of T4 to T12 vertebrae	*Upper fibres:* lateral third of clavicle *Middle fibres:* acromium and upper border of spine of scapula *Lower fibres:* medial portion of crest of spine of scapula (tubercle)
Rhomboid muscles – major and minor	Adducts (retracts) and draws scapula towards spinal column; rotates scapula downwards	Spinous processes last cervical (C7) vertebra and first five (T1–5) thoracic vertebrae	Medial border of scapula below spine
Serratus anterior	Abducts (protracts) scapula; rotates scapula upwards (Stabilises scapula when hand exerts pressure on an object, as in press-ups)	Ribs 1–9 at side of chest	Anterior surface of medial border of scapula
Pectoralis Minor	Abducts (protracts) and draws scapula laterally away from spinal column; draws scapula forward and downward	Anterior surfaces of ribs 3–5	Coracoid process

Table 3.3 Muscles that move the shoulder joint (attach to the humerus)

Muscle	Actions	Origins	Insertions
Latissimus dorsi	Extends arm from flexed position; adducts arm from abducted position; internal rotation; horizontal abduction	Posterior crest of ilium, spinous processes of lumbar and lower six thoracic vertebrae, back of sacrum, lower three ribs	Medial side of bicipital groove of humerus
Teres major	Extends shoulder; internal rotation; assists in adduction and medial rotation of arm	Inferior third of lateral border of scapula	Medial lip of bicipital groove of humerus
Deltoid	*Anterior fibres:* abduct, flex, horizontally adduct and internally rotate shoulder

Middle fibres: abduct shoulder

Posterior fibres: abduct, extend, horizontally abduct and externally rotate shoulder | *Anterior fibres:* anterior border and superior surface of lateral third of clavicle
Middle fibres: lateral border of acromium process
Posterior fibres: inferior border of spine of scapula | Deltoid tuberosity, on lateral surface of humerus |
| Pectoralis major | *Upper fibres:* internal rotation, horizontal adduction, flexion, abduction after 90° and adduction of the shoulder
Lower fibres: internal rotation, horizontal adduction, extension and adduction of the shoulder | Medial half of clavicle, Sternum and upper six costal cartilages | Lateral lip of bicipital groove of humerus below greater tubercle of humerus |

Table 3.3 cont.

Muscle	Actions	Origins	Insertions
Coracobrachialis	Flexes, adducts and horizontally adducts shoulder	Coracoid process	Middle of medial border of humeral shaft
Rotator cuff muscles			
Supraspinatus	Weak abduction and stabilisation of humeral head in glenoid cavity	Medial two-thirds of supraspinatus fossa	Superior aspect of greater tubercle of humerus
Infraspinatus	External rotation; horizontal abduction; extension of shoulder; stabilises humeral head within glenoid cavity	Medial aspect of the infraspinatus fossa just below spine of scapula	Posterior aspect on greater tubercle of humerus
Teres minor	External rotation; horizontal abduction; extension of shoulder; stabilises humeral head within glenoid cavity	Posteriorly on upper and middle aspects of lateral border of scapula	Posterior aspect on greater tubercle of humerus
Subscapularis	Internal rotation; adduction and extension of shoulder; stabilises humeral head in glenoid cavity	Entire anterior surface of subscapular fossa	Lesser anterior tubercle of humerus

Table 3.4 Muscles that move the neck

Muscle	Actions	Origins	Insertions
Sternocleidomastoid	*Both:* side flexion *Right:* rotation to left and lateral flexion to right *Left:* opposite	Manubriuim of sternum, medial clavicle	Mastoid process
Scalenes (anterior, medius, and posterior)	Raises first and second ribs, flexes and rotates neck	Transverse processes of C2 to C6	Upper surfaces of first and second ribs

Table 3.5 Muscles that move the forearm and wrist

Muscle	Actions	Origins	Insertions
Biceps brachii	Flexes elbow and supinates forearm; flexes shoulder	*Long head:* supraglenoid tubercle of scapula *Short head:* coracoid process of scapula	Tuberosity of radius and bicipital aponeurosis
Brachialis	Flexes elbow	Distal half of anterior portion of humerus	Coronoid process of ulna
Brachoradialis	Flexes elbow; pronates forearm from supinated position to neutral; supinates forearm from pronated position to neutral	Distal two-thirds of lateral condyloid ridge of humerus	Lateral surface of distal end of radius at styloid process
Triceps brachii	*All heads:* extends elbow *Long head:* extends and adducts shoulder	*Long head:* infraglenoid tubercle of scapula *Lateral head:* upper half of posterior surface of humerus *Medial head:* distal two-thirds of posterior surface of the humerus	Olecranon process of ulna
Anconeus	Extends elbow	Posterior surface of lateral condyle of humerus	Posterior surface of olecranon process of ulna
Pronator teres	Pronates forearm; flexes elbow	Distal part of medial condyloid ridge of humerus and medial side of ulna	Middle third of lateral surface of radius
Pronator quadratus	Pronates forearm	Distal anterior aspect of ulna	Distal anterior aspect of radius

Table 3.5 cont.

Muscle	Actions	Origins	Insertions
Supinator	Supinates forearm	Lateral condyloid ridge of humerus and neighbouring posterior aspect of ulna	Lateral surface of proximal radius
Extensor digitorum	Extends wrist; extends second to fifth phalanges at meta-carpophalangeal joints	Lateral epicondyle of humerus	Four tendons to bases of mid and distal phalanges of four fingers
Extensor carpi radialis brevis and longus	Extends and abducts wrist	Lateral epicondyle of humerus	Base of second and third metacarpals
Extensor carpi ulnaris	Extends wrist; adducts wrist with flexor carpi ulnaris	Lateral epicondule of humerus	Base of fifth metacarpal
Flexor carpi radialis	Flexes and abducts wrist	Medial epicondule of humerus	Base of second and metacarpals
Flexor carpi ulnaris	Flexes wrist; adducts wrist with extensor carpi ulnaris	Medial epicondyle of humerus and posterior aspect of proximal ulna	Base of fifth metacarpal, pisiform and hamate
Palmaris longus	Flexes wrist	Medial epicondule of humerus	Palmar aponeurosis of second to fifth meta-carpals

Table 3.6 Muscles that move the trunk

Muscle	Actions	Origins	Insertions
Rectus abdominis	*Both sides:* lumbar flexion *Right side:* lateral flexion to right *Left side:* lateral flexion to left	Crest of pubis	Cartilage of ribs 5–7 and xiphoid process
External obliques	*Both sides:* lumbar flexion *Right side:* lumbar lateral flexion to right; rotation to left *Left side:* lumbar lateral flexion to left; rotation to right	Borders of lower eight ribs at side of chest, dovetailing with serratus anterior	Anterior half of crest of ilium, inguinal ligament, crest of pubis, fascia of rectus abdominis muscle at lower front
Internal obliques	Lumbar flexion; lumbar side flexion; lumbar rotation	Upper half of inguinal ligament; anterior two-thirds of iliac crest and lumbar fascia	Costal cartilages of ribs 8–10 and linea alba
Transversus abdominus	Compresses abdomen	Outer third of inguinal ligament, inner rim of iliac crest, cartilage of lower six ribs and lumbar fascia	Crest of pubis and iliopectineal line, abdominal aproneurosis to linea alba
Quadratus lumborum	Contraction of one side bends vertebral column laterally (side flexion to the side it is located); stabilises pelvis and lumbar spine; major stabiliser of lower back working with psoas	Posterior inner lip of iliac crest	Approximately half length of lower border of twelfth rib and transverse process and upper four lumbar vertebrae
Erector spinae (includes iliocostalis – lateral layer; longissimus – middle layer; spinalis – medial layer)	Extension and lateral flexion of spine	Various	Various

Table 3.7 Muscles that move the hip

Muscle	Actions	Origins	Insertions
Iliopsoas	Hip flexion; external rotation of femur. Psoas is a major stabiliser of the lower back, working in conjunction with quadratus lumborum	*Iliacus:* inner surface of ilium *Psoas:* lower borders of lumbar vertebrae, sides of last thoracic vertebra (T12), and base of sacrum	Lesser trochanter of femur and shaft below, pectineal line and iliopectineal eminence
Sartorius	Flexes, abducts and rotates femur laterally; flexes knee	Anterior superior iliac spine and notch just below spine	Anterior medial condyle of tibia
Rectus femoris	Extends knee; flexes hip (*see also* Table 3.8)	Anterior inferior iliac spine of ilium and superior margin of acetabulum	Superior aspect of patella and patellar tendon to tibial tuberosity
Tensor fascia latae	Abducts and flexes hip. Tendency to rotate hip internally as it flexes	Anterior iliac crest and surface of ilium just below crest	Upper part of iliotibial tract on femur
Piriformis	Externally rotates hip	Anterior sacrum, posterior portions of ischium, and obturator foramen	Superior and posterior aspect of greater trochanter
Piriformis as above with Gemellus superior and inferior, Obturator externus and internus, Quadratus femoris	Group of six lateral rotators sometimes known as the piriformis group		
Gluteus maximus	*Upper:* abducts and laterally rotates thigh *Lower:* extends and rotates thigh laterally	Posterior of crest of ilium, posterior surface of sacrum and coccyx near ilium, and fascia of lumbar area	Oblique ridge on lateral surface of greater trochanter and iliotibial band

Table 3.7 cont.

Muscle	Actions	Origins	Insertions
Gluteus medius	Abducts hip; externally rotates as hip abducts; internally rotates (anterior fibres)	Outer surface of ilium	Posterior and middle surfaces of greater trochanter of femur
Gluteus minimus	Abducts hip; internally rotates as hip abducts	Lateral surface of ilium	Anterior surface of greater trochanter of femur
Biceps femoris	Flexes knee; extends hip (*see also* Table 3.8)	*Long head:* ischial tuberosity *Short head:* lower half of linea aspera, and lateral condyloid ridge	Lateral condyle of tibia and head of fibula
Semitendinosus	Flexes knee; extends hip (*see also* Table 3.8)	Ischial tuberosity	Upper anterior medial surface of tibia
Semimenbranosus	Flexes knee; extends hip (*see also* Table 3.8)	Ischial tuberosity	Posteromedial surface of medial tibial condyle
Pectineus	Flexes, adducts and internally rotates hip	Front of pubis just above crest	Rough line from greater trochanter to linea aspera on anterior aspect
Adductor longus	Adducts and medially rotates thigh; assists in hip flexion	Anterior pubis just below its crest	Middle third of the linea aspera
Adductor brevis	Adducts and externally rotates hip	Front of inferior pubic ramus just below the origin of the longus	Lower two-thirds of pectineal line of femur and upper half of medial lip of linea aspera
Adductor magnus	Adducts and externally rotates hip	Edge of entire ramus of pubis and ischium and ischial tuberosity	Whole length of linea aspera, inner condyloid ridge and adductor
Gracilis	Adducts and internally rotates hip; flexes knee	Inner edge of descending ramus of pubis	Anterior medial surface of tibia below condyle

Table 3.8 Muscles that move the knee

Muscle	Actions	Origins	Insertions
Popliteus	Flexes and internally rotates knee	Posterior surface of lateral femoral condyle	Upper posterior medial surface of tibia
Quadriceps			
Rectus femoris	Extends knee, flexes hip (*see also* Table 3.7)	Anterior inferior iliac spine of ilium and superior margin of acetabalum	Superior aspect of patella and patellar tendon to tibial tuberosity
Vastus lateralis	Extends knee	Anterior and inferior borders of greater trochanter, gluteal tuberosity, upper half of linea aspera and entire lateral intermuscular septum	Lateral border of patella, patellar tendon to tibial tuberosity
Vastus medialis	Extends knee	Whole length of linea aspera and medial condyloid ridge	Medial half of upper border of patella and patella tendon to tibial tuberosity
Vastus intermedius	Extends knee	Upper two-thirds of anterior surface of femur	Upper border of patella and patellar tendon to tibial tuberosity
Hamstrings			
Biceps femoris	Flexes knee; extends hip (*see also* Table 3.7)	*Long head:* ischial tuberosity *Short head:* lower half of linea aspera, and lateral condyloid ridge	Lateral condyle of tibia and head of fibula
Semitendinosus	Flexes knee; extends hip (*see also* Table 3.7)	Ischial tuberosity	Uppera anterior medial surface of tibia
Semimembranosus	Flexes knee; extends hip (*see also* Table 3.7)	Ischial tuberosity	Posteromedial surface of medial tibial condyle

Table 3.9 Muscles that move the ankle and foot

Muscle	Actions	Origins	Insertions
Gastrocnemius	Plantarflexes foot; flexes knee	*Medial head:* posterior surface of medial femoral condule *Lateral head:* posterior surface of lateral femoral condyle	Posterior surface of calcaneus (Achilles tendon)
Soleus	Plantarflexes foot	Posterior surface of proximal fibula and proximal tibial surface	Posterior surface of calcaneus (Achilles tendon)
Tibialis posterior	Plantarflexes and inverts foot	Posterior surface of upper half of interosseus membrane and adjacent surfaces of tibia and fibula	Lower inner surfaces of navicular bones and bases of second to fifth metatarsal bones
Flexor digitorum longus	Plantarflexes four toes and ankle; inverts foot	Lower two-thirds of posterior tibia	Base of distal phalanx of four toes
Flexor hallucis longus	Plantarflexes big toe and ankle; inverts foot	Lower two-thirds of posterior fibula	Base of distal phalanx of big toe (plantar surface)
Tibialis anterior	Dorsiflexes and inverts foot	Upper two-thirds of lateral surface of tibia	Inner surface of medial cuneiform and first metatarsal
Extensor digitorum longus	Extends four lesser toes; dorsiflexes ankle and evert foot	Lateral condyle of tibia, head of fibula, anterior upper two thirds of fibula	Middle and distal phalanges of lesser four toes (dorsal aspect)
Extensor hallucis longus	Dorsiflexes big toe and ankle	Middle two-thirds of medial surface of anterior fibula	Base of distal phalanx of big toe (dorsal aspect
Peroneus longus	Everts foot and plantarflexes ankle	Head and upper two-thirds of lateral surface of tibia	Under surfaces of medial cuneiform and first metatarsal

Table 3.9 cont.

Muscle	Actions	Origins	Insertions
Peroneus brevis	Everts foot and plantarflexes ankle	Lower two-thirds of lateral surface of tibia	Tuberosity of fifth metatarsal bone
Peroneus tertius	Everts foot and dorsiflexes ankle	Distal third of anterior fibula	Base of fifth metatarsal
Plantaris (absent in some humans)	Plantarflexes ankle; flexes knee	Lateral supracondylar ridge of femur	Posterior surface of calcaneus

Ageing and regeneration of muscle tissue

Skeletal muscle fibres do not have the ability to divide, and thus growth can only come from the enlargement of existing cells (*hypertrophy*) and not from any increase in the number of fibres (*hyperplasia*). Skeletal muscle fibres grow by incorporating more *satellite cell* nuclei within them. Satellite cells represent left-over embryonic cells that formed the muscle fibres in the first place; this process cannot replace large areas of tissue and so can only help with subtle repair. Extensive damage to skeletal muscle fibres can only be replaced by *fibrous scar tissue*. Chapter 12 on injury management discusses the healing process of injured skeletal tissue and the role of scar tissue in this process.

Cardiac muscle fibres do not have the ability to divide or be replaced, and can only be healed by the formation of scar tissue. Smooth muscle fibres can increase by hypertrophy, and in some areas may also divide and grow by hyperplasia.

Conditions affecting the muscular system

♦ *Cramp* – contrary to popular belief, cramping is not due to dehydration and salt deficiency; body salt concentration increases with dehydration. While the precise causes of cramp remain unclear (the link between dehydration and cramping is not conclusive), factors which interfere with the circulation probably contribute to the condition, such as tight socks, tight shoes, the accumulation of lactic acid and cold weather.

♦ *Delayed onset muscle soreness (DOMS)* – this is a soreness that develops in muscles about 24 hours after unaccustomed exercise. It can last for about three days and normally resolves itself. There are different theories on the causes of DOMS. One of the latest is that it involves disruption of what is called the *cytoskeleton* of muscle fibres, which is vital for harnessing the muscle contraction and transferring it to the tendon – but more research is needed to confirm or disprove this. An earlier theory suggesting that DOMS is caused by lactic acid production has been dismissed.

♦ *Fibrosis* – the formation of fibrous connective tissue in areas where it is not normally found. It is often formed following an injury.

♦ *Muscular dystrophies* – hereditary, muscle-destroying diseases usually affecting skeletal muscle fibres, which cause progressive weakening and reduction in muscle mass. The most common is Duchenne muscular dystrophy, which is now known to result from a defective gene for a muscle protein called dystrophin.

♦ *Multiple Sclerosis* – a disease caused by the progressive destruction of the myelin sheaths of neurons in the central nervous system, often causing the patient to lose the ability to contract skeletal muscle in various parts of the body.

♦ *Myalgia* – a general term used to describe pain in muscles.

♦ *Myasthenia gravis* – a rare autoimmune disease in which the patient's own antibodies attack the neuromuscular junction or motor end plate.

♦ *Myoma* – refers to any tumour that is composed of muscle tissue.

♦ *Myomalacia* – the softening of muscle tissue.

♦ *Myopathy* – refers to any disease of muscle tissue.

♦ *Myositis* – the inflammation of muscle fibres.

♦ *Myotonia* – increased muscle tone, or tonic spasm. This occurs when the excitability of muscles increases, causing them to relax more slowly after contracting.

♦ *Paralysis* – the loss of nervous functions, usually motor, resulting in the inability to stimulate muscle contraction.

♦ *Spasm* – the sudden, involuntary contraction of groups of muscles. Asthma is believed to be the spasm of the muscular coats of the smaller bronchi.

♦ *Stitch* – thought to be caused by tension of the diaphragm, commonly experienced during exercise or after eating a large meal.

♦ *Tenosynovitis* – an inflammation affecting tendons, and their synovial sheaths.

♦ *Tremor* – a rhythmic, involuntary contraction of opposing groups of muscles.

♦ *Wryneck* – a spasm of the deep muscles of the neck, causing twisting of the neck and an unnatural position of the head.

♦ Other systems relevant ♦ to sports massage

The cardiovascular system

This involves the workings of the heart and blood vessels. By understanding how it works, the sports massage therapist may influence circulation through massage and seek to advise clients on how to improve functioning and therefore physical performance.

The heart is a muscular organ that beats rhythmically by unconscious stimulation from the brain for someone's lifetime. Its function is to force blood through a system of vessels (arteries and arterioles) to all tissues throughout the body. The blood in the arteries and arterioles carries nutrients and oxygen to the tissues, and then carries waste products, such as carbon dioxide, via venules back to the lungs and the heart. Blood is prevented from flowing back through the veins by a series of valves, and blood flow to the heart is aided by muscular contraction. Hence inactive or bed-bound patients are more vulnerable to circulatory problems.

The *lymphatic system* is a secondary system of capillary vessels running parallel to the vascular system. It is responsible for the removal of excess tissue fluid that has leaked from the terminal blood vessels as nutrients are exchanged between blood and tissues. When the tissue fluid seeps into the lymphatic vessels it is called *lymph*, and is carried by these vessels – via regional lymph nodes – to large veins in the neck where it is added to the blood again. The lymph nodes are important filters that can remove harmful materials and produce antibodies to aid in the body's defence against infection.

The respiratory system

The lungs are responsible for the exchange of gases between the body and the environment. Air is drawn in through the mouth and nose as the diaphragm contracts and/or the rib cage expands. It travels via a series of passages that decrease in size, until it reaches small sacs in the lungs called *alveoli*. The walls of these sacs are only one cell thick, and this allows the oxygen to permeate through the cell lining into the bloodstream. At the same time, carbon dioxide is expelled from the alveoli.

The respiratory and cardiovascular systems are important for aerobic exercise, which uses energy derived from glycogen (from the blood supply) and oxygen (from the lungs). It is the effective functioning of these two systems, often collectively called the *cardio-respiratory system*, that sustains normal everyday activities.

The digestive system

The digestive system processes ingested food during its passage through the alimentary canal. This includes both solids and – important for athletes – fluids. The right balance of food is essential in providing basic nutrients such as carbohydrates for energy, proteins to help build and repair tissue, and fats for adequate neurological and hormonal development. While a correct diet alone will not make an athlete perform better, it is essential for maintaining health and in providing sufficient fuel to meet the demands of exercise. Since one of the main aims of the sports massage therapist is to help clients optimise performance, understanding what fuels the body needs most, and how easily they are absorbed allows the therapist to give general advice on diet in relation to exercise. However, clients affected by medical conditions resulting from, or affected by, food intake should be referred to a specialist.

The nervous system

The nervous system transmits a constant series of messages via electrical impulses to and from the control centre situated in the brain. These messages are either receiving information from various tissues via the sensory nerves, or initiating the actions of other tissues, such as organs, muscles, etc. Messages stimulating action fall into two categories: *conscious*, whereby a conscious thought is required to bring about an action such as moving a limb; and *unconscious*, such as the constant stimuli required for the heart to beat without conscious thought. These messages travel via a system of nerves to the spinal cord, which leads to the brain.

Sports massage therapists use specific techniques to stimulate a clients' sense of touch to influence their physical and psychological state (as discussed in Chapter 5). By understanding how the nervous system functions we can appreciate how these messages are transmitted and how they interact with the muscular system. This is important as each system not only interacts with, but also affects, how the other functions. For example, a very tight muscle may compress a nerve passing through it. This may slow down the nerve impulses travelling through it, and in turn slow down the functioning of the muscle.

Chapter 4

Exercise and the human body

To understand how sports massage plays a role in maintaining fitness we need to look at the impact of physical exercise on the body's systems. Chapter 1 briefly describes how an athlete uses a programme of progressive overload to specific areas of activity, so that the body gradually adapts to the increased stress and thereby becomes stronger, faster, etc. It also considers how sports massage can help in this process, by helping the body recover, releasing muscle tension and so on (*see* p. 2). This chapter examines the components of fitness, the body's energy systems, the factors that influence an athlete's performance, and the effects of exercise on the human body.

The type, intensity, and duration of each massage session should be tailored specifically to the demands of the athlete in relation to their physical condition, training, competition and so on, at that specific point in time. By understanding more about the physiological changes that take place within the body as a result of exercise, the sports massage therapist is better able both to assess a client, and to optimise the benefits of sports massage for them.

◆ The components of ◆ fitness

Fitness may be defined as the ability to carry out functional or sporting activities for a prolonged period in the absence of pain or discomfort*. When assessing an athlete's fitness for a particular activity, you need to consider the five 'S' components:

◆ Speed
◆ Skill
◆ Stamina
◆ Suppleness
◆ Strength

How each of these components are developed depends on the demands of an athlete's sport or activity. For example, a shot putter may spend more time developing strength and skill than, say, a squash player, who may concentrate more on speed and suppleness. However, all areas must be considered, no matter what the sport, to ensure a balanced exercise programme.

*This definition may be used to measure fitness, although it is recognised that strenuous activity leading to fitness gains is often 'uncomfortable'. This should however always be controlled and never excessive.

♦ What factors affect ability ♦ to exercise?

Body shape

There are three basic types of physique, called somatotypes. These somatotypes also tend to differ in terms of body composition – the proportion of lean body tissue (muscles, organs and blood) and body fat (adipose tissue) – and these differences influence an athlete's suitability for particular sports and activities. Figure 4.1 illustrates the following somatotypes:

♦ *Ectomorphs* – tend to be thin, with low muscle and fat levels.
♦ *Endomorphs* – are more rounded in shape, and have higher body-fat levels, than ectomorphs.
♦ *Mesomorphs* – are in between the former two types, with a high proportion of muscle and corresponding bone mass. They are best suited to strength training and body-building programmes; however, all body types are able to increase muscle size to some extent with appropriate training.

Age

Age is an important consideration in determining the type and level of physical activity to which an individual is suited. Studies have shown that humans tend to do less physical activity as they grow older, and with advances in technology, many aspects of everyday life are now much less physically demanding. Even as early as the mid-twenties, metabolic rate may begin to slow down. *Metabolism* is a collective term describing all the complex chemical changes that take place in the body, enabling it to function. These changes either break down substances into simpler ones, or build others up to more complex ones. At the same time, energy is either released or consumed accordingly in each process. *Metabolic rate* is the rate at which energy is expended for the body to function; it increases during physical exertion, stress, fear and illness, and may slow as we begin to age.

In addition to a slowing of our metabolic rate, muscles and connective tissue become less supple and reflex actions become slower. The onset of these processes, however, is *very*

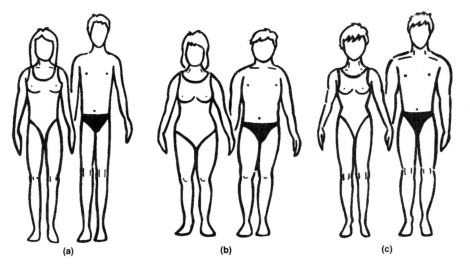

Figure 4.1 Somatotypes – the three basic types of physique: (a) ectomorph; (b) endomorph; (c) mesomorph

slow and may be slowed even further by regular exercise. The most obvious deterioration in muscle mass occurs in the over fifties and approximately 10 per cent of muscle mass is lost in each subsequent decade. However, recent evidence has shown that people over 80 can successfully undergo training programmes to increase strength and improve balance.

Medical conditions

Medical conditions do not automatically preclude an athlete from sport or physical activities. People suffering from conditions such as asthma and diabetes are able to participate in sport, many at competitive levels. However, the sports massage therapist needs to check for and identify any conditions and should seek medical advice wherever necessary.

Nutrition

The right intake of food from a healthy, balanced diet will provide the correct fuel needed for exercise and the growth and maintenance of body tissue. Athletes are most vulnerable to injury and illness when they are training the hardest and the body's immune system is depleted. Poor diet during periods of strenuous exercise will increase the risk of injury due to the weakening of the structures in the body. For more information on this subject, see *The Complete Guide to Sports Nutrition* by Anita Bean (A & C Black).

Fluid intake

Fluid intake before and during exercise is crucial for sustaining physical activity at an optimum level. It is estimated that a 5 per cent fall in body fluid will lead to a 20 per cent reduction in performance levels. Thirst indicates that the effects of dehydration have already begun; drinking at this stage is too late. Correct fluid intake is a combination of the right type, the right amount and the right time before, during and after training and competition. An athlete's requirements must be individually tailored and to take into account the type and intensity of the sport, climate and temperature, duration of the event, etc.

♦ The body's energy ♦ systems

To understand the effects of exercise on the body's systems we need to look at how the body creates energy for exercise, and how the different forms of exercise place different demands on energy production. The main energy systems of the body can be defined as: the *aerobic* system, the *anaerobic lactic* and *anaerobic alactic* systems. The aerobic system functions with oxygen, the anaerobic lactic functions with oxygen and produces lactic acid (*see* below) as a by-product, and the anaerobic alactic functions without oxygen but does not produce lactic acid as a by-product. It is convenient to describe the systems as separate concepts; however, during actual exercise all three systems interweave to produce the desired performance outcome. All three systems involve the breakdown of a substance called *adenosine triphosphate* (ATP) to *adenosine diphosphate* (ADP), releasing energy in the form of mechanical action and heat (*see* also pp. 25–6). Anyone who has worked up a good sweat on a brisk run will appreciate that 65 per cent of the energy is heat, while only 35 per cent is converted to activity.

Aerobic energy and exercise

Aerobic exercise is physical activity involving energy utilised in the presence of oxygen. Examples of aerobic exercise are long-distance swimming, running, rowing, etc.

When a person works aerobically they are usually working below 75 per cent of their maximum heart rate* using energy produced from carbohydrates, fats and proteins stored in the body. The other major factor affecting the use of aerobic energy is the transportation, uptake and utilisation of oxygen, which depends on the efficiency and capacity of the respiratory system (*see* p. 41). Effects of aerobic exercise in improving oxygen use are described later in this chapter.

For moderate activity the preferred fuel is carbohydrate, stored in the form of *muscle glycogen*. Sugars and starches from the diet are broken down and absorbed by the body, and released into the bloodstream as glucose which is then stored in the muscle cells as glycogen. The hormone insulin plays an important role in the transfer of blood glucose into muscle glycogen. When the activity is low in intensity but very long in duration, fats are the preferred fuel source. Fats, excess sugars and starches, and excess proteins are all broken down and absorbed by the body and released into the bloodstream as triglycerides. The triglycerides are transported in the bloodstream through mechanisms related to cholesterol and deposited in adipose tissue stores throughout the body. Adipose tissue is what we commonly refer to as body fat.

Aerobic exercise relies extensively on slow-twitch fibres, which are discussed in Chapter 3. Studies have shown that training does not change the proportion of slow- and fast-twitch fibres within muscle, so that athletes will always find it difficult to change from their more favoured explosive sport to an endurance sport or vice versa. However, more recent studies suggest that many years of endurance training can result in some fast-twitch fibres (type IIA) taking on the characteristics of slow-twitch fibres.

The aerobic system is the most complex form of energy production. The advantage is its high ouptut of energy, yielding 38 molecules of ATP from one molecule of glucose. When the fuel being oxidised (or 'burned') is fat, energy production is much higher; for example, one molecule of the relatively common free fatty acid, *palamatic acid*, will produce 129 molecules of ATP. Under extreme stress the body will consume protein as a metabolic fuel source; however, this requires the breakdown of muscle or organ tissue and is not generally recommended.

Anaerobic lactic energy and exercise

Anaerobic exercise is physical activity of a short duration – from three seconds to about three minutes – using energy produced without oxygen. Any exercise of an explosive nature utilises the anaerobic energy system, for example sprinting, shot put or boxing. It also produces the lactic acid that causes discomfort in the muscles during high-intensity exercise (*see* below).

The anaerobic lactic energy system involves the breakdown of glucose or glycogen to pyruvic acid, a process referred to as *glycolysis*. Without oxygen this becomes lactic acid, which stops the energy production. This process can only last in its purest form for up to 45 seconds and produces two or three molecules of ATP (glucose yields two, while glycogen yields three). Any sport involving a large number of 'stop-start' intervals utilises this system, for example tennis, netball and volleyball.

---

*May be defined as the highest heart rate possible for an individual during any given exercise modality. There are different ways of calculating this rate – which is strongly influenced by age and fitness level.

Anaerobic alactic energy and exercise

Also known as the ATP-PCr system, this is the simplest of the three energy systems. In addition to ATP there is a second molecule present called *phosphocreatine* (PCr.) This is used to restore ADP to ATP without the presence of oxygen. PCr keeps the production of ATP constant – however, supplies of PCr exhaust very quickly (after about 3–10 seconds during times of high muscular intensity).

♦ The effects of exercise ♦ on the human body

Effects on the muscular system

Muscular adaptations to exercise can be viewed as changes in the components of muscular fitness: *strength, endurance* and *flexibility*. Major changes in local muscular endurance are largely related to improved delivery and utilisation of oxygen within the cells; as such, it will be considered as an adjunct to cardiorespiratory fitness – described below as cardiorespiratory peripheral adaptations. Stretching and its effects on flexibility are covered in Chapter 11. An introduction to 'strength conditioning', or adaptations in muscular strength in relation to resistance training*, follows.

Strength conditioning does more than increase muscular strength and size: motor neuron activity is enhanced, resulting in greater contractility and co-ordination; connective tissue is strengthened; and a general sense of wellbeing can be found when previously difficult tasks become effortless.

*Resistance training involves increasing strength by way of muscular contractions against a force – or gravity.

The first two effects are considered below, while the last is best experienced for one's self!

Resistance exercise may increase the size of the working muscle through a process known as *hypertrophy*. There are two types of hypertrophy that can occur with resistance training: *transient hypertrophy* and *chronic hypertrophy*. Transient hypertrophy refers to the 'pumping up' of the muscle during a single exercise session. This is due, initially, to increased blood perfusion in the working muscle and, later in the workout, to the loss of fluid from blood plasma and its accumulation in the intracellular spaces of the muscle. This condition only lasts a short time because the fluid is returned to the blood within hours.

Chronic hypertrophy refers to the increase in muscle size that occurs as a result of long-term resistance training. This is brought about by the structural change within the muscle as the protein myofilaments suffer microtrauma and the body adapts by laying down additional protein to repair the damage. This is the basis of the principle of overload and recovery (*see* also Chapter 1, p. 2). While the number of muscle fibres is believed to remain constant, the fibre itself may show an increase in not only the mass of existing myofibrils, but also in the number of myofibrils and sarcomeres.

Fast-twitch fibres respond more visibly to resistance training than slow-twitch fibres. Type IIA and IIB fibres both exhibit cross-sectional growth in response to resistance training when the stimulus is high enough. Type I fibres will have an initial cross-sectional increase related to increased protein synthesis, but this is limited in extent. Much of the increase in Type I muscle size is related to increased vascular proliferation (an increase in the capillary network supplying the muscle tissue) and mitchondrial numbers within the muscle unit and cells. Increases in Type I fibre mass follow low-intensity, high-repetition training sessions – sessions which are insufficient to stimulate large changes in Type II fibre. Someone with a greater proportion of fast-twitch fibres will, therefore, have more of a tendency to add muscle bulk under conditions of high-intensity workloads.

The popular bodybuilding media have grasped a hold of inconclusive evidence to suggest that *hyperplasia* – or increased muscle fibre numbers – is due to auto-generation or muscle fibre splitting. There is evidence to suggest that this occurs in some animal species; there is no conclusive evidence reporting occurrences in human subjects.

The functional benefits of the increased cross-sectional area of muscle fibres and strength gains are:

♦ a greater ability to exert force;
♦ improved balance, co-ordination and gait;
♦ increased ability to perform activities of daily living;
♦ enhanced high-level athletic performance.

Effects on the cardiorespiratory system

Cardiorespiratory adaptations to exercise are numerous. As they deal with the changes in the intake, transport and utilisation of oxygen, they encompass adaptations in the heart, lungs, vascular tissue and muscles.

Central adaptations can best be defined as *an increase in cardiac output,* or the amount of blood that can be circulated around the body. Cardiac output is the product of *stroke volume* and *heart rate.* Maximal heart rate is not trainable; indeed, well-trained athletes may exhibit a drop in maximal heart rate due to training. As a client ages, their maximal heart rate will slowly decline – although exercise may attenuate the decline. Stroke volume, therefore, is the largest determinant in the variability of an individual's cardiac output, and is explained below.

As a person trains, the heart is effectively exercised. The left ventricle, which pumps blood into the systemic circulation, will begin to strengthen and enlarge. Both the thickness and strength of the myocardium (the muscular wall of the heart) and the volume of the left ventricle (or chamber) will increase. The myocardium not only gets stronger, it also gets more pliable, and with this increased pliability it is able to expand more fully before contraction – increasing volume yet again. With increased force of contraction more blood is ejected from the ventricle, leaving a reduced residual volume. All told, the volume of each stroke is greatly enhanced from increased pre-fill and ejection and decreased end-volume.

Pulmonorespiratory, or lung and breathing, function is seldom the limiting factor to exercise capacity in healthy clients. Exercise adaptations are more noticeable during exercise than at rest, with increases in efficiency of between 20 and 30 per cent over pre-training levels.

Peripheral adaptations can best be defined as an improvement in the working tissue's ability to extract oxygen from the circulating blood. This is due to an increase in capillary bed density (the number of small blood vessels supplying the tissues) and mitochondria numbers within the muscle cells. The increased capillary density has a three-fold effect:

♦ the rate of dispersion through each individual capillary is reduced as a given volume of blood circulates through more capillaries;
♦ the distance from each capillary to an adjacent muscle cell is decreased;
♦ the surface area over which the oxygen can diffuse is increased.

Slow-moving blood, close to an increased area of the muscle cell membrane, is more likely to release its oxygen to the muscle and its mitochondria.

Metabolic adaptations include increased ability to control the accumulation of metabolic wastes, especially lactic acid, in the system before they begin to have a detrimental effect on performance. Type of training will determine whether the body is becoming more adept at functioning without producing higher levels of lactic acid, or whether the body has become efficient at its removal. There is also evidence to suggest that aerobic exercise will encourage an enzymatic change in Type IIA fibres, causing them to act in a manner mimicking Type I fibres.

The combination of central and peripheral adaptations described above brings about an increase in maximal aerobic power or VO_2 max, which is defined as the body's highest rate of sustainable oxygen consumption during exercise.

Effects on the nervous system

Neurological adaptations to exercise are difficult to measure directly. However, it is recognised that resistance training enhances the increases synchronisation of the recruitment. This is noted in the increase in power output and co-ordination, independent of changes in the muscle tissue itself.

Good co-ordination and balance is vital for any athlete: the quicker the reactions, the greater the chance of having a edge on the opposition, or of improving a personal best. The nervous system can be trained and improved with repetitive exercises. New and extended movements involving nerve action may be progressively learned, practised and perfected.

Research has shown that as a result of the physiological changes brought about by regular exercise, the mental agility and attitude of a person are affected in a very positive manner. A person will usually feel more alert and more positive following exercise (*see* also below, on beta-endorphins).

When rehabilitating an injured part, it is often beneficial to exercise and stimulate the symmetrically uninjured part as well. To some extent, nerves serving muscles under our conscious control work in pairs – so the effects of training a muscle or limb on one side of the body may be passed on to the muscle or limb on the other side of the body.

Effects on the skeletal system

Mechanical stresses from exercise may improve bone condition. These stresses are imposed by skeletal muscle pulling at its origins and insertions, weight-bearing activities and gravity. It has been shown that in the areas of the skeleton where these stresses are applied the most, more mineral salts are deposited and more collagen fibres are produced, causing both the density and size of bone to increase. This supposition is borne out by the greater bone mass observed in weightlifters than in endurance athletes such as joggers, and in racquet players, who have shown greater bone density in their playing arms. This knowledge and its use in planning appropriate exercise may help prevent the possible onset of osteoporosis, particularly in women (*see* pp. 20–1). Equally, a lack of exercise and its effects provide further evidence: it has been shown that if a fractured leg is immobilised by being placed in plaster, after only a few weeks the bone becomes decalcified and weakened in the absence of mechanical stresses.

Effects on the digestive system

Most types of exercise have a positive effect on the digestive system by helping to suppress appetite and increase metabolism.

The suppression of appetite for a period following activity may be due to the effects of exercise on the autonomic nervous system, or an increase in body temperature, or both.

Appetite may be defined as 'the desire to eat food for a pleasant sensation, based on a satisfying previous experience'. As such, it is possible to accept that the exercise-related release of *beta-endorphins* (the body's natural morphine associated with 'runner's high') will produce a state of relaxation that will preclude the desire to eat for pleasure.

The effect of exercise on appetite helps to regulate food intake – and therefore to balance energy requirements with more controlled intake and more efficient energy production from an increase in metabolism. Conversely, exercise burns more calories than its sedentary alternatives – requiring more food (largely carbohydrates) to be consumed for metabolic fuels. As long as there is a balance between calories burned and calories consumed, weight gain will not result.

A second benefit of exercise is the resultant increase in rate of through-put in the large intestine and rectum. Research has related increased rates of through-put, whether from increased exercise or increased dietary fibre, to lowered incidences of colonic cancers. Some types of exercise however, especially endurance events, can sometimes cause an upset stomach or runner's diarrhoea.

Chapter 5

The principles of sports massage

Massage aims to produce three types of effect on the body systems: *physical, physiological* and *psychological*. While these effects are closely interrelated, it is the initial physical effects brought about by the manual skills of a massage therapist that lead to the physiological and psychological effects. Hence, the stroking, squeezing, compression, rubbing, etc. that is applied to the skin and underlying muscles produce not only physical benefits, but also triggers physiological and psychological responses in the body. To achieve the desired balance and results it is vital to understand the principles behind the various massage techniques. The type and extent of their effect on the body depends on the technique itself, the depth to which it is applied, and the area of the body being massaged. The techniques referred to in this chapter are described in detail in Chapter 9.

♦ Physical effects of ♦ sports massage

Stretches soft tissue

Muscle fibres are able to contract and therefore have good extensibility. Most of the restriction in the flexibility of a muscle derives from the connective tissue that surrounds the muscle and the muscle fibres (*see* also pp. 23–4). Rigorous massage movements, such as kneading and wringing, stretch and loosen the skin and underlying tissue. This is achieved by the therapist's hands applying force on the surface in various ways, to push and pull the soft tissues. Other benefits of the massage, such as increased blood circulation and temperature, help the tissues become more pliable. With the additional forces applied, parallel muscle fibres may be separated, the connective tissue which surrounds them stretched, and the fibres stretched longitudinally. This all helps restore flexibility and separate adhesions.

Relieves muscle tension

The sports massage therapist needs to determine whether a muscle is in an unusually tense state or whether it is merely inflexible (*see* below), before deciding on appropriate techniques. The therapist may be able to feel which it is, as soon as they palpate the area (*see* also Chapter 8); alternatively, it will become obvious according to how the tissue reacts to the massage.

Muscle tension may be reduced by simple stroking actions that stimulate the peripheral nerve receptors. These receptors are nerve endings situated in the skin and underlying fascia which detect changes in the environment and transmit messages via the nervous system to the brain where we perceive these changes as conscious feeling. Such changes in the environment may relate to temperature, pain, pressure and so on. These stimuli often create a response in the underlying muscles. For example, extreme cold causes rapid involuntary contractions (shivering), thereby creating heat to warm the body. Depending on the stimulus, the response may be for the muscle tension to increase or for muscles to relax. This is a reflex action, as distinct from the use of mechanical forces to stretch muscle fibres and connective tissues, as described above. We can now understand how discomfort or pain during massage would cause muscles to tighten up, while stroking movements help relax them.

Improves flexibility of muscle

Studies* have shown that massage aimed at muscle relaxation can result in an increased range of motion in a joint (*see* also Chapter 3, p. 17). Muscles span joints, and are able to contract and so draw their origins and insertions closer together and reduce the angle of a joint. If individual muscles and/or groups of muscles are encouraged to relax, this has a direct effect in extending the limit to which the affected joint or joints can move.

Reduces muscle spasm

Muscle spasm is an extreme level of tension in the muscle, usually brought about by the body's protective mechanism resulting from pain. The body reacts by contracting muscles to prevent further movement. (This is discussed in more detail in Chapter 6, under *Musculo-skeletal imbalances*). As described

above, even with extreme levels of tension, massage can help to relax the muscle and increase mobility.

Improves formation of scar tissue

Frictions (*see* Chapter 8, pp. 83–4) applied across the overall direction of the muscle fibres ('cross-fibre') to a specific area may be used to separate fibres which may have adhered together as a result of some form of strain or minor tear. Similar actions may be used more aggressively to break down scar tissue and encourage the alignment of new scar tissue with the direction of the existing muscle fibres. (*See* Chapter 12 for more information on massage and injuries.)

Reduces swelling

Swelling may be caused by blood which has leaked out from torn blood vessels, or by fluids moving through the capillary walls into interstitial spaces. By massaging the area, an increase in movement and temperature within the soft tissues will increase lymph flow – leading to fluids being reabsorbed into the circulatory system (*see* also p. 40.

Note: While many claims can be made and substantiated about the effects of sports massage, there is no evidence to suggest that there are any techniques which will increase the strength of a muscle (i.e. bring about hypertrophy) – nor is there any truth in massage being able to reduce fatty tissue!

*Nordschow and Bierdian (1962), 'Influence of manual massage on muscle relaxation: effect on trunk flexion', *Physical Therapy*, **42**, pp. 653–6.
Bell (1964), 'Massage and the physiotherapist', *Physiotherapy* (JCSP), **50**, pp. 406–8.

♦ Physiological effects of ♦ sports massage

Increases blood and lymph flow

Localised blood circulation may be improved as a result of sports massage. As the depth and pressure of the massage increases, so does the probability that the deep blood vessels are compressed and released, stimulating circulation. Massaging a limb using deep stroking and kneading can also increase blood flow to the opposing limb. This is especially beneficial for an athlete who has an immobilised limb as a result of a fracture, for example – or for partially-abled athletes (*see* Chapter 12 for more information on massage and injuries).

Prolonged massage has been demonstrated to increase lymph flow from the area being massaged through the lymph glands towards the heart. Increased lymph flow from the extremities may be best stimulated by deep stroking and kneading techniques. It is also known that lymphatic drainage is influenced by gravity; elevating the limb may therefore enhance the effects of sports massage on lymph flow.

Increases supply of oxygen and nutrients to the soft tissue

Just as blood flow may be increased as a result of appropriate forms of massage, scientific experiments* show that the haemoglobin and red cell count may also increase. Combined with an increase in blood and lymph flow, this leads to an improved supply of oxygen and nutrients to the soft tissue.

*For example, Perberton, R. (1950), 'Physiology of massage,' in *A.M.A. Handbook of Physical Medicine and Rehabilitation* (Philadelphia: Blakiston).

Removes waste products

As lymph flow increases as a result of massage, waste products from areas of soft tissue may be reabsorbed via the lymphatic system into the circulatory system.

Relieves pain

There are a number of reflex actions that the therapist can induce which will have a sedative effect on the client or a relaxing effect on specific muscles. One of these effects, which has a significant role to play in sports massage, is pain relief. Pain generated in an area is perceived by messages travelling to the brain via afferent nerves (sensory nerves, usually with receptors at the skin and joints). Pain relief works on the principle of the 'pain-gate theory'. It is known that rubbing the painful area stimulates the cutaneous mechanoreceptors (sensory nerve endings situated in the skin), creating afferent signals that block the transmission of the pain signals to the spinal cord. As the messages do not reach the brain, the perception of pain is reduced.

Stimulates the nervous system

It is generally accepted that massage has various effects on the peripheral and central nervous systems, although these effects are not necessarily supported by scientific evidence. The theory is that stimulation of the nervous system may also be a major factor contributing to an increase in blood circulation and temperature – which brings about increased muscle elasticity, and delivers fresh nutrients and oxygen to the muscles.

◆ Psychological effects of ◆ sports massage

Relieves tension and anxiety

Massage should for the most part be a pleasant experience. Therefore, as clients learn this, the expectation often leads to them being in a more relaxed mental state before the massage begins. There is also a considerable overlap between the physiological and the psychological. For example, it is more difficult to achieve muscular relaxation without a conscious effort being made to relax mentally at the same time. In this way the neurological stimulus to muscles may be minimised. Consider the reverse. Someone who remains in an anxious state is likely to have much greater muscular tension, with the consequent energy expenditure leading to fatigue more rapidly.

In short, the pleasant feeling (physiological response) of appropriate massage techniques helps with the process of mentally 'letting go' (psychological response), which in turn helps the muscles relax. So it is impossible to separate the physiological and psychological effects of massage, and easy to see how a cycle between the two is initiated during massage. Massage therefore may be considered to help with physical relaxation and relief of tension and anxiety.

Pain relief

Massage may also be used for pain relief. This is because by stimulating mechanoreceptors in the skin, the afferent signals block the transmission – and therefore the perception – of nociceptive (pain) signals. Once again, by using massage to effect physiological change, the psychological perception of pain will also be altered. This obviously plays an important role when dealing with injury management and rehabilitation.

Stimulates physical activity

Just as you can bring about a relaxed state, so too can you alter the pace and intensity of a massage to stimulate the athlete and encourage physical activity. The sports massage therapist must assess their client's physical and mental state before deciding on an appropriate approach. For example, a competitor who is already tense and anxious needs to be relaxed with slower techniques, whilst others already relaxed need quicker movements to produce an invigorating effect. Pre-competition massage, for example, can incorporate brisk, light movements to stimulate the athlete psychologically as well as physiologically (*see* also Chapter 10, p. 114).

Chapter 6

How sports massage may enhance performance

Chapter 5 discussed the physical, physiological and psychological benefits of sports massage. This chapter explains how these effects may translate into measurable benefits to the athlete in terms of performance levels for both training and competition.

A major role of the sports massage therapist is to *educate* their clients. This involves having some knowledge of other areas which may affect their level of activity and sporting performance, but which are not always directly related to the activity itself. Lifestyle, occupation and diet are just some of the things which can influence our state of physical and mental wellbeing – which in turn determines how well we respond to the demands of rigorous activity. Such factors may have short-term as well as long-term effects.

The following text therefore considers the factors which can influence a client's physical and mental state; what effects these factors may have on performance; what may be done to change those influences, where appropriate; and when the sports massage therapist might profitably 'intervene'.

♦ Promotes recovery and ♦ prevents overuse

Chapter 1 discussed how a training schedule to improve performance is based on the principles of overload and overcompensation, whereby the body is subjected to gradual increases in physical stress. Following rigorous exercise, microscopic changes take place to blood vessels, connective tissue and muscle fibres. This is the start of the adaptation process and relies on sufficient time for proper recovery following controlled periods of activity.

This managed and gradual increase in the stresses placed on the body allows and encourages adaptations in the soft tissue to cope with greater levels of activity aimed at specific needs. The recovery period and the speed with which these physiological changes take place during this time are important to the success of the programme and in helping the person to remain healthy. If the overload is increased too quickly, or too little time is allowed for recovery before the next bout of exercise ensues, the microscopic changes do not happen quickly enough to cope. Instead of adaptation, the muscle fibres may become irritated and inflamed, and muscles may respond by becoming tighter. If this cycle is repeated often enough the effects of what is commonly known as 'overuse' develop, and these often lead to imbalances in the musculoskeletal system described in more detail later in this chapter. If ignored and allowed to become chronic, they will not only hinder the athlete's rate of improvement, but in many cases performance will suffer and injury result. Figure 6.1 illustrates a typical overuse/injury cycle which perpetuates unless broken by an appropriate combination of rest and/or sports massage.

Massage is an important means of helping muscles recover from fatigue. By increasing blood and lymph circulation, waste products resulting from exercise are removed more efficiently and the supply of nutrients to the muscles is enhanced. This may help recovery and speed up the training adaptations, thereby helping to prevent overuse.

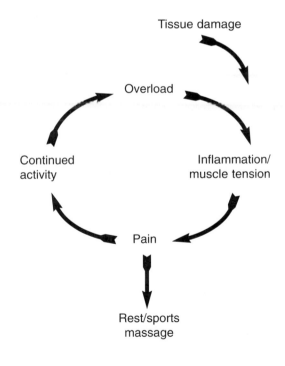

Figure 6.1 A typical overuse/injury cycle

Helps prevent injury

One of the most important benefits of sports massage is the prevention of injury by helping to maintain healthy muscles. If an athlete, for whatever reason, has tight muscles that are not able to function at their best, their chances of suffering injury – either as a result of overuse, as described above, or a more serious traumatic injury increase. For example, in contact sports where agility is an important means of defence, a player with restricted agility might suffer an injury from an unexpected tackle or impaired co-ordination. These injuries may be traumatic, such as a muscle tear.

Promotes healing

Since an injured person is usually less mobile, their metabolism and the associated healing processes slow down. Sports massage stimulates the healing process by warming the tissues and increasing blood flow, so that the blood vessels become dilated and the capillary walls more permeable. This allows better transportation of nutrients and oxygen to the affected tissues and removal of waste products from the area, thereby speeding up the repair process. The correct techniques used after the acute phase may also encourage better alignment of new scar tissue in the direction of existing muscle fibres (this is discussed further under *Injury management* in Chapter 12).

Restores mobility

Massage helps restore flexibility to the muscles and joint range of motion by reducing muscle tension caused by the body's protective mechanism following injury (*see* text on musculo-skeletal imbalances, below).

This induces relaxation, and separates muscle fibres and adhesions caused by injury or occurring in unusually tight – or relatively inactive – muscles.

Promotes confidence

By helping an athlete relax mentally you will also have a positive effect on their confidence and their preparation for competitions. This relaxed state and sense of wellbeing may reduce tension and anxiety.

♦ Musculo-skeletal ♦ imbalances

Maintaining healthy muscles helps prevent injury, but it is not sufficient to address problems with individual muscles or muscle groups without looking at the body as a whole. This is because parts of the body do not work independently without affecting other areas. Chapter 3 discussed the skeletal and muscular systems, showing how the skeleton is the framework that maintains our shape and provides points of attachment for muscles, and how the muscles contract and relax to create movement of the joints in the skeleton. These two body systems are often referred to as one system – the *musculo-skeletal* system – because of the way in which the bones and muscles interact and function together. The various parts of this system are interdependent: a muscle contraction in one area will have an effect on the state of tension in many other muscles, tendons and ligaments throughout the body. Likewise, a weakness or undue tension in one part of the system will inevitably have an effect on the rest of the system.

For example, if an athlete strains the rotator cuff muscles in their shoulder playing tennis, the body may respond by increasing the tension in those and surrounding muscles in order to limit movement and protect the area from further injury. This is one of the body's protective mechanisms. The problem at this stage may be minor, so the athlete continues playing on a regular basis without treatment. As they do so, however, they start altering the way in which they strike the ball – this may be an unconscious action due to the tightened muscles in the shoulder, or it may be a conscious action to avoid discomfort. As the tension continues and the striking action alters, secondary effects begin to take place: muscles in the shoulder and back start working to compensate, posture may be affected, and in the long term the athlete's gait may change.

Once such a cycle is set up, the problem is compounded. The athlete, believing the strain to be minor and one which may be overcome without treatment, perseveres with their sport or activity. . .and in an effort to do so, exacerbates the problem. They may alleviate it by stretching to release some of the tension, or they may rest to allow time for proper recovery. Unfortunately, minor problems often go untreated until more serious damage is inflicted – for example, when an unusually tight muscle cannot withstand the strain of a poorly co-ordinated movement during a game. Even if a serious injury does not occur, the athlete's musculo-skeletal system will be affected and their performance will continue to suffer. If the imbalance becomes chronic, muscles, tendons and connective tissue adapt, leading to shorter muscle lengths, reduced flexibility, and poorer range of motion.

Summarising the effects of musclo-skeletal imbalances

The range of possible effects of muscle imbalances may be summarised as follows (the word 'changes' being used to describe 'aberrations from the norm' for an individual):

- increased strain on muscles, tendons, ligaments and bone;
- changes in soft tissue development;
- changes in skeletal development (for chronic imbalances);
- reduced flexibility and range of motion;
- muscle wasting, or atrophy;
- changes in strength;
- changes in reflex actions;
- changes in conscious action;
- discomfort or pain;
- changes in emotion;
- poorer posture;
- poorer performance.

Hereditary imbalances may be permanent, and therefore – although symmetrical differences may be observed – these will have become the 'norm' for such a person. In this instance, further changes are less likely to take place.

What are the possible causes of musculo-skeletal imbalances?

These are often subtle and difficult to detect, as an affected athlete may not be able to recall when or how the problem first appeared. The sports massage therapist should consider each of the following probable causes.

Environment
Environment includes the athlete's lifestyle, surroundings and occupation. Do they have an office job and sit at a desk all day, or does their daily routine include physical work? Do they spend many hours driving?

Environmental factors may have a greater influence over an athlete's physical state than their sport or activity, particularly if they spend many more hours per day working. As technology advances, jobs are becoming more specialised and less varied. You may need to check the way in which your client sits at a desk, uses a computer, drives a car, lifts equipment, etc. A simple act such as sitting with a wallet in the back pocket, or carrying a bag over one shoulder, can start off minor imbalances that can become chronic.

Stress
Most people have to deal with some pressure on a daily basis. At times the intensity of such pressure increases and the ability to cope with everyday tasks diminishes. This emotional stress (as opposed to physical) often translates into tight muscles and postural problems. Persistent stress can also lead to weaknesses and problems in other body systems, often resulting in some form of illness.

Type of physical activity
Find out about your client's sport or exercise programme. Very few physical activities are well balanced. Most favour one side of the body, which will set up imbalances: you usually find the favoured side of the body is stronger and has more muscle bulk. This can also lead to poorer range of motion in the affected joints. Peripheral physical activities or sports, especially when played infrequently, may also have a bearing on an individual's physical condition.

Posture
Postural problems often result from secondary causes, such as environmental factors (*see* above). However, they may be due simply to development of bad habits. Check how your client sits and positions him or herself. Do the things they do at work affect their posture? Stress may also influence posture.

Hereditary

Sometimes, for all the checking and history-taking, there simply may not be any satisfactory explanation for imbalances and the problem may have existed since birth.

Illness

Anyone who has endured even a short period of bed-rest due to illness is likely to suffer after-effects. Apart from feeling fatigued, the muscles may have weakened, atrophied and stiffened due to inactivity, all of which may affect an athlete's posture and gait.

Injury

Traumatic injury has many effects on the human body, some of which have already been discussed briefly in the introduction to this section. First, the body responds by protecting the site of injury. Movement becomes more painful, partly because the soft tissue – now swollen with additional fluid – is less supple, and partly because any movement increases the pressure on the sensory nerve endings. Increased muscle tension or even spasm will also limit the movement of an affected area.

These reactions will have both physiological and physical effects on the surrounding muscles. Increased pressure will impede blood vessels and neural pathways to the muscles, limiting the supplies of nerve impulses, blood, oxygen and nutrients, as well as the removal of waste products. Muscles that remain inactive will start to waste or atrophy; they will become inflexible, and the muscle fibres and connective tissue will soon shorten. Muscle strength and power will be lost and joints affected by these muscles will not reach their full range of motion. The body will begin to compensate for these weaknesses and loss of function.

How long do imbalances take to develop?

This varies according to both the cause of the imbalance and the area or areas of the body affected. Some imbalances may develop gradually over many weeks, months, or even years; others can occur in much more dramatic fashion – such as in the following case study.

Case study

A rugby player who was recovering from a minor shoulder injury decided to maintain his fitness by road running. As he was not used to this type of running, the repeated impact of his feet on hard ground and stress from carrying his considerable stature resulted in unusually tight calves. During treatment for his calves, he revealed that he was also suffering 'twinges' in his back. An examination indicated muscle spasm and marked scoliosis (or exaggerated lateral curvature) of the spine. This had all developed in just two weeks. Because there had been little time for any long-term tissue changes or problems to develop, after two sessions of sports massage and the removal of road running from his programme he was virtually back to normal.

For the rugby player, the probable cause of the imbalance was quite plain. Other problems that take much longer to appear and have no obvious cause are much more difficult to unravel.

Do all imbalances need to be corrected?

People do not fall apart from minor imbalances. The sports massage therapist needs to try and determine whether an imbalance is having any ill-effects, or whether trying to correct them – particularly after a long period – will cause worse problems. After all, if a client appears to have been carrying an imbalance for a long time, their body may be very well adapted to coping with it.

Imbalances are often extremely subtle in their early stages, and test the powers of perception and palpatory skills of the sports massage therapist to the full. The sports massage therapist must therefore always keep an open mind to all possibilities while using these skills. The gravity of the effects of such imbalances may not always be apparent, either to the client or the therapist – so that careful questioning, examination, palpation and assessment are needed (often over a series of sports massage sessions) before a clear progression becomes more obvious. In particular, any observations and changes must be noted down: record-keeping is discussed in the following chapter.

PART THREE

Putting theory into practice

Chapter 7

Examining and assessing your client

This chapter will discuss what happens in the initial consultation: the importance of client history and record-keeping, how and what to communicate to the client, and the physical assessment. All these skills are as crucial to getting good results as the massage itself. For the purposes of this text, the word 'examination' is used to describe the process of *observation* and subsequent note-taking, etc.; and the word 'assessment' to describe the process of *drawing conclusions* from such observation. (In reality, of course, there are no distinct boundaries – the processes are interrelated.)

♦ Client history and ♦ record-keeping

Before the massage

Recording your client's history is often the only means of assessing their needs. As such, this process is an important part of the first consultation and should include the following essential information:

- the type of sport or physical activity in which they are involved;
- the level at which they are involved – i.e. club, county or country; or novice, semi-competitive, elite;
- frequency of training/competition;
- any previous injuries;
- any previous and/or current medical conditions, including any current medication.

A pre-printed record card is the most efficient and time-saving method of recording these and other details. It is important to keep the history concise and not to spend too long getting all the information down on the record card. After all, your client has come to you to enjoy the benefits of sports massage, not to spend too long answering questions that they might consider unnecessary. Figure 7.1 (*see* opposite) shows an example of a record card. The headings provide you with a starting point for the questions that you need to ask. The answers will often focus your attention on the areas that need to be explored further.

CONFIDENTIAL   Referred by _____

Name _____ Occupation _____

Tel: Day _____ Eve _____ Mob _____ D.O.B. ___/___/___

Address _____

Sex: M/F _____ Exercise & frequency _____

Other activities _____

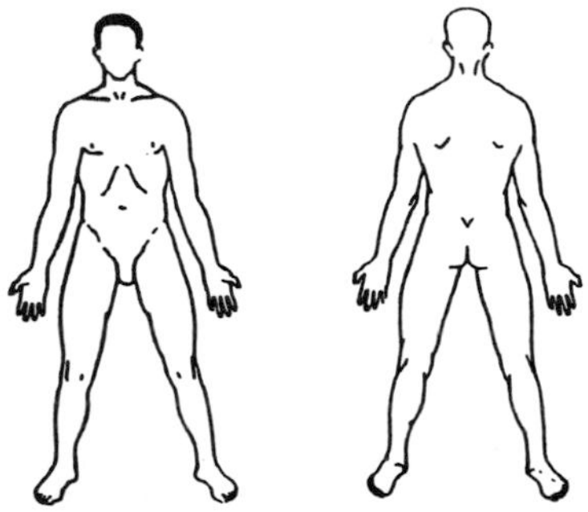

History _____

_____

_____

_____

_____

_____

_____

_____

_____

_____

Medication _____

Copyright - Academy of Sports Therapy

Features of Pain: Main area _____

Radiating _____ Character _____ Severity _____

Duration _____ Frequency _____ Times of commencement _____

Other factors _____

Date	Fee	Notes

Copyright - Academy of Sports Therapy

Figure 7.1 A sample record card

It is essential that you review your client's history before any subsequent massage, so that you can remind yourself of any conditions which may influence the effects of massage – and adjust the session accordingly.

During and after the massage

During and after each massage session you should note down the type of massage and advice given to your client. This will enable you to assess their progress, and make informed decisions on further treatment. In addition, if you ever have the misfortune of being accused of causing a problem, or making one worse, a detailed record of the information you received from your client, and the massage and advice given, will be essential reference. Luckily this rarely happens, particularly to those who have been properly trained and who work within the limitations of their training (*see* also Chapter 2, p. 6). Professional indemnity insurance policies (*see* Chapter 2, p. 7), often carry requirements for written records which must be kept pertaining to each client.

How much information do I need to record?

As a therapist, you will not want to read a short essay every time your client returns for massage. You need to be able to read key points or symbols that focus your attention on any important areas. These key points should provide the stimulus for you to remember any other background.

Anatomical drawings and symbols are a useful way of recording and recalling information and will often tell you much more than wordy sentences. Simply mark the drawing with a cross or shaded area to record any tight muscles or problem areas. Symbols can also be used to add information. There are a variety of symbols that you can formulate to meet your own needs, but here are just two examples that are commonly used:

> Improving
< Problem getting worse

All recorded information must remain confidential between you and your client, and record cards in a place accessible only to you.

How do I put my client at ease?

Psychologically, if you can reduce any anxiety perceived by your client this is likely to enhance the physical state of relaxation. As discussed in Chapter 5, these are closely interrelated, each having a strong influence on the other. Your confidence and ability to put your client at ease and the way in which you behave will influence the way they feel – and thus enhance the benefit of the massage. Your client must be fully confident in you as a therapist. Any anxiety at this stage will inevitably make your job more difficult when you begin to massage.

Equally, the way in which you encourage a client to perceive specific aspects of treatment – and indeed, their own physical state – can have a profound effect on them and on the success of your massage. If you spend too long focusing on a minor muscle strain, will your client become over-anxious? On the other hand, if you do not give it enough attention, will your client regard the problem as insignificant and make it worse by continuing a rigorous training programme?

There are various ways of putting a client at ease, depending on both the therapist and the client. However, there are some common guidelines that are useful in any situation. A sports massage therapist needs to be reasonably relaxed, cheerful, interested in their client, and confident in their approach.

At the initial assessment, always begin by introducing yourself and welcoming your client by name. Even though the client may have spoken to you on the phone, they may need a reminder of your name and this gets them 'off the hook' in case they have forgotten. You may then go on by saying, for example, 'Now when we spoke over the phone yesterday, you said you had overdone your training and had particularly tight calves as a result. How are they today?' After your client has replied, you may go on to explain that you would first like to take a few notes before beginning the massage. Advising the client that you are going to do this, and explaining why, reassures them – and, in turn, gives them the opportunity to ask anything they need to about your notes, such as confidentiality (*see* above).

Now you can start to ask the questions prompted by your record card. Introduce the questions in a conversational style, not simply in a military fashion such as 'Name? Occupation?', etc. While acknowledging each reply, be careful not to waste time on conversation which digresses from your history-taking and the relevant facts – you can return to various topics later while massaging.

Is there anything else I should tell them before the massage?

Yes, tell them what they can expect from the session. By now they have told you why they need sports massage, so this is another opportunity to reflect on what you have heard and to set out what you plan to do and hope to achieve. However, don't make promises or guarantees. Remember that at this stage, you have not felt the tissues or confirmed any expectations you might have from the history; anything too definite now may be premature and end in disappointment. A brief and general statement is appropriate, such as the following:

As your main reason for the massage today is to try and sort out your tight calves, that is where I'll start. I will also work on the rest of both legs to see if there have been any knock-on effects, and finally I will return to the calves before we finish to do some more work on loosening them up. After that perhaps we can chat about stretching and your exercise programme to see if there are ways in which we might help prevent this recurring – is that okay?

This is reassuring to the client: they know what to expect and a sort of informal contract is established for what you hope will be achieved during the session. If you don't tell your client what to expect, you may face a problem when you advise them that you have finished – and they ask for another area to be massaged. If you have another client waiting and so politely refuse, your first client may leave feeling disgruntled.

Now you must advise your client clearly on how much to undress, and how you would like them to be positioned on the couch. It is very important that you explain this clearly and concisely to keep them 'at ease'. Perhaps something like the following:

In a moment I would like you to undress to your underwear and lay face down, with your head at this end of the couch and your feet over this cushion. I will put this towel over you to keep you warm and then I'll explain the rest as we go along, okay?'

It is appropriate for you then to busy yourself with record cards, oils, and so on – averting your eyes away from your client until you are aware that they are ready on the couch. At such a time you can step forwards and place a bath-sized towel over them.

♦ After the first massage ♦

If you can encourage your client to receive sports massage on a frequent basis, they will be able to experience the long-term benefits for their training and performance. One of the keys to the success of the massage is ensuring that other exercise-related activities are being carried out correctly. Sports massage is beneficial, but much more so when received in combination with appropriate exercise, stretching, rest, competition, etc.

Discuss your client's training priorities, short-term and long-term goals. By understanding these you will be able to work together towards the same goals. Then find out who else may be involved in their treatment, such as injury-care specialists, coaches and trainers. You may well need to liaise with them for the benefit of your client. Once you have established common goals you can begin to plan your strategy with your client, and share with them your plans and suggestions for further consultations. By following all of these guidelines your client will realise that you are committed to the same goals and have an interest in helping them succeed.

Be careful when planning and giving advice to a client that it remains within the scope of a sports massage therapist: the real drive to get them through strenuous training sessions or competitions is the responsibility of the coach, and you should not try to fulfil this role.

Finally, you need to dictate the timing of the next appointment. If it is too far ahead, the benefits of the first session will be lost; the client may forget your recommendations and lose motivation and interest. Once you have discussed what they are aiming for and enlightened them on how sports massage may help in future sessions, it is easy to follow on by saying something like:

> If your next major race is in 10 days, I would like to see you four days from now to see if your calves have stayed loose after this massage, and then we can discuss whether to see you again before the race or wait until after. So let's see, four days is Friday, how does that suit you?

While it is your professional duty to recommend what is best for your client based on your knowledge of sports massage, if you are not succeeding in your approach within a reasonable number of appointments you should refer them to another specialist for advice. This may be a physiotherapist or osteopath, who may be better trained in assessing biomechanical dysfunction and the reasons for it.

How can I encourage my clients to follow my recommendations?

To help your clients remember what they need to do after the massage, ask them to write down what they do each day and what results they get. This way, the client feels more obliged to follow your recommendations – and the information you receive at the next session is likely to be more comprehensive than a verbal report.

How do I make sure any advice I give does not conflict with other sports therapy professionals?

Following a massage session you may need to advise your client on a number of aspects of their training programme: for example, how they stretch, how much rest they need, what they may need to avoid. If there are other specialists involved, such as a coach, trainer, physiotherapist or sports doctor, you must consult with them either by phone or in person, to ensure that your advice will not conflict with other treatment and will not be detrimental to your client.

If there is a coach or trainer involved, ask your client for their telephone number so that you can speak to them – or find out when training sessions are being held so that you can meet them. You can then explain your planned programme of treatment, and at the same time reassure the coach that they will be consulted first if there is any potential conflict. This will give the coach the comfort of knowing that you are not 'interfering', nor will you 'interfere' with the athlete's usual routines without contacting them first.

♦ The physical examination ♦

Why do I need to do a physical examination?

With each client you need to gather as much information as possible about his or her overall condition. There are many different ways to assess a client's physical condition, visually as well as by touch, and the more information you have at your disposal the more accurate will be your assessment. During the initial part of the consultation, while you are recording the client's history (*see* p. 60), you will gain clues about their current and past state of health, and the effects this might have had on their body. Once you have completed this, you may decide there is a need to carry out a physical examination as well. A physical examination can involve:

♦ observing the person while they are standing in a relaxed position and assessing their posture, muscle bulk, and alignment;
♦ testing the range of motion of certain joints;
♦ testing and comparing the strength of muscles on each side of the body.

The results from such an examination will give you a more complete picture of your client's physical state. Once you have gathered this information you are then able to decide on the best form of massage to suit your client's needs. Once you start to massage your client, you should find that any differences in muscle tone, muscle bulk, etc. match your initial assessment.

How much time do I spend on the physical examination?

There are so many means of examining and checking a client's physical condition that you could easily spend an entire massage session assessing posture, muscle definition, joint function and strength. Although it is important to gather detailed background information, you must never lose sight of the purpose of your client's visit – the sports massage. They may not take kindly to spending a lot of time being assessed, rather than massaged; they may also be fit and healthy, and not require an extensive physical examination.

For the client's first visit, you should first carry out an overall observation of the body just to complete the picture. Then, if their history includes details of injuries, or their type of work suggests they may have

65

musculo-skeletal imbalances (see pp. 56–9), you may check specific joints for range of motion and muscles for strength to determine whether there are any problems. At the same time, any problems identified should be checked to determine their seriousness. There is no need to check the entire body; it would take far too long would not necessarily improve the quality of the massage.

In respect of follow-up visits, you should already have a good record of your client's background and physical condition. So, after a brief consultation and discussion, you may need to check specific areas to see whether there have been any changes since the last visit, and then proceed with the massage.

The physical examination is ideally done with the client in a standing position, but in many working environments there may not be enough space to perform this task effectively. Many treatment rooms have little spare space in which a client may satisfactorily be observed – this needs to be done from immediately behind the client, from about a metre away in a well-lit area. In such instances the sports massage therapist has to make do with observing and 'examining' their client in a relaxed state, lying down.

After a lot of practice in observing posture and symmetry, it will take you only two or three minutes to examine your client and record any abnormalities. Any other functional checks may be carried out as necessary.

How do I check alignment and muscle bulk?

The client should be dressed in under-garments only (*see* pp. 62–3 for advice on how to achieve this without discomfort to your client), so that you can fully observe all bony prominences and surface areas. (These bony prominences are visible landmarks on the body from areas of bone which can be seen under the skin. They are described more fully in Chapter 8 – *see* p. 77). Put your client at ease by telling them what you intend to do. Then ask them to stand with their feet three to four inches apart, shoulders relaxed and arms by their sides. Try to get them to stand in a well-lit area where there are no shadows which might make observation difficult and assessment inaccurate.

There are many different ways of observing and assessing a client for alignment and muscle bulk. The following is a method of assessment which can be used when looking at the client from behind. (When palpation is mentioned in the text, you may need to refer to Chapter 8 for a description of this technique and advice on how to carry it out.) You need to practise this routine so that the whole process does not take long and your notes are concise. You will not wish your client to become uncomfortable and to start wondering why the examination has taken so long – they may conclude that there are a lot of things wrong with them!

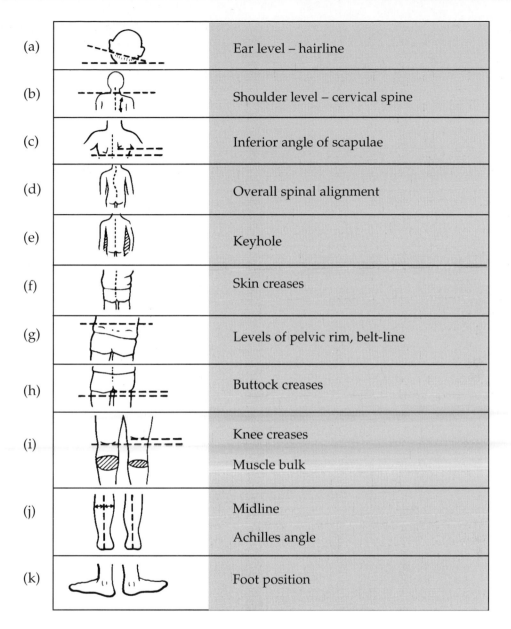

(a)	Ear level – hairline
(b)	Shoulder level – cervical spine
(c)	Inferior angle of scapulae
(d)	Overall spinal alignment
(e)	Keyhole
(f)	Skin creases
(g)	Levels of pelvic rim, belt-line
(h)	Buttock creases
(i)	Knee creases / Muscle bulk
(j)	Midline / Achilles angle
(k)	Foot position

Figure 7.2 Examination of the client from behind

Examination from behind

Stand about a metre away from your client. If you stand too close you will not be able to compare each half of the body effectively. An imaginary vertical line running from the head to between the feet should divide the body into two halves.

Head

Begin by looking at the head to see if it is level. Use landmarks such as the hairline (depending on the haircut) and the ears. Try not to align the ears with the shoulders in case the shoulders are not level (*see* Figure 7.2(a))

Shoulders

Next look at the shoulders and see if they are level. Do this by observing the level of the bony prominences of the acromio-clavicular joints (*see* Figure 7.2(b)) relative to the level of the cervical spine. Also look for differences in muscle bulk. If the upper fibres of the trapezius are more developed on one side it can make the shoulders appear uneven, and it's important not to confuse the two.

Also check the alignment of the inferior angle of the scapulae (*see* Figure 7.2(c)). How easy this will be will depend on the amount of soft tissue lying over the scapulae. If necessary ask your client to abduct their arms and you will see the scapulae swinging. You may also need to step forwards and palpate for each bony prominence.

Back

Look at the spinous processes running from the belt-line to the neck and see if they form a vertical line (*see* Figure 7.2(d)). If these bony prominences are not easy to observe, ask the client to slowly ease the palms of their hand down the fronts of their thighs so that the shoulders slump forwards and the spine flexes. This will make the spinous processes stand out and allow you to assess the spinal alignment. In this position (*see* Figure 7.2(e)) any bending of the spine (scoliosis) becomes more obvious. Another clue is to look at the number of skin creases on each side of the body around the midriff (*see* Figure 7.2(f)). If there are more on one side than the other, this will indicate that the person is tending to lean to one side.

Now check what is known as the *keyhole*, which is the gap between the arms and the body (*see* figure 7.2(e)). Any differences will usually tie in with a misalignment of the shoulders or spine.

Pelvis

To check whether the pelvis is level, look at the belt-line of the client's undergarment as your first clue (*see* Figure 7.2(g)). Then move forwards and palpate for the posterior superior iliac spines, looking and feeling to judge if they are in a horizontal plane. Next look at the creases between the buttocks and the top of the hamstrings and look for any discrepancies between the two, which will indicate that the pelvis is not level (*see* Figure 7.2(h)).

Legs

Look at the backs of the knees and compare the skin creases to see both the number of creases and their angles (*see* Figure 7.2(i)). These are an indication of the amount of muscle bulk in the hamstrings and the calves.

Now check the vertical alignment of the Achilles tendons and whether there is any thickening of either tendon (*see* Figure 7.2(j)). Any differences here will almost certainly correspond with your assessment of the feet.

Feet

Look at the angle of the feet while the client is standing in a relaxed position (*see* Figure 7.2(k)). Look at their arches and any areas of particularly hard skin around the feet. You may also choose to ask your client to walk, to confirm whether they are over-pronating or over-supinating.

How do I check posture?

Posture is observed from the side. In an ideal posture there should be an imaginary vertical line, called the *plumb-line*, running from the ear through the cervical vertebrae, shoulder joint, lumbar vertebrae, hip, midline of the knee and down to the lateral malleolus (*see* Figure 7.3). Any deviations from this line will tell you about the condition of the back and pelvic tilt. (*See* also Chapter 3, p. 21, for illustrations of spinal curvatures.)

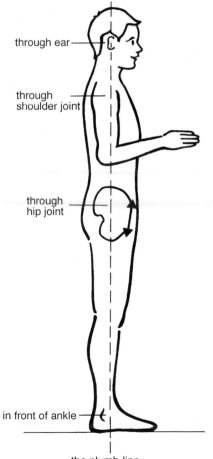

through ear

through shoulder joint

through hip joint

in front of ankle

the plumb-line

Figure 7.3 The plumb-line

How do I check range of motion?

Range of motion (ROM) is the amount of movement that can be achieved without discomfort to a joint. Chapter 3 covered all the possible joint movements in the body. Once these are understood, checking and comparing range of motion becomes easier. Most joints produce more than one movement, so there may be several ranges to check.

There are accepted standards of ROM for each joint, which you will learn with experience, but this text will concentrate on comparing one side to the other. If both sides appear limited, your own knowledge of joint range will help you decide whether they are impaired or not.

Table 7.4 includes a list of actions for checking the range of motion of joints in the human body. When instructing your client, give clear directions so that they avoid vigorous or jerky movements. Remember to use layman's terms to relate the movement to your client and, if necessary, demonstrate to make things clear.

How do you test for strength?

Strength-testing specific muscles requires extensive study and practice, and the information provided below is intended only as a brief introduction to the subject. You need to learn about muscles – their origins, insertions, and muscle actions – and then you need to practise so you can understand the best positioning of the body to isolate and contract each muscle. To help you learn, think about which muscles are working when you are exercising in a gym, or what are the repetitive actions when playing a particular sport.

Once you understand how to get a particular muscle to contract, instruct your client to contract against your resistance for

Table 7.4 Testing joint range of motion (ROM)

Neck		Trunk	
Flexion	Chin to chest	*Flexion*	Slump forwards (from standing), bending whole spine
Extension	Raise chin up and look at the ceiling	*Extension*	Return to upright and arch back
Side rotation	Turn head to the side, left then right	*Rotation*	Gently twist spine by simultaneously moving one shoulder backwards and one forwards keeping pelvis still – left then right
Side flexion	Move ear towards shoulder, left then right		
Shoulder girdle			
Elevation	Raise shoulders		
Depression	Lower shoulders		
Protraction	Bring shoulders forwards		
Retraction	Push shoulders back	*Side flexion*	Side bend, left then right
Shoulders		**Hips**	
Flexion	Move arms forwards	*Flexion*	Bring upper leg forwards
Extension	Move arms backwards	*Extension*	Move upper leg backwards
Abduction	Move arms outwards	*Abduction*	Move leg to the side and away from the body
Adduction	Move arms inwards		
Elbows		*Adduction*	Move leg inwards towards the body
Flexion	Bend elbow		
Extension	Straighten elbow		
Forearms		**Knees**	
Supination	Turn palm upwards	*Flexion*	Bend the knee
Pronation	Turn palm downwards	*Extension*	Straighten the knee
Wrists		**Ankles**	
Flexion	Bend wrist, fingers move towards palmar surface of forearm	*Plantarflexion*	Move foot to point toes downwards
Extension	Straighten wrist, fingers move away from forearm	*Dorsiflexion*	Move foot to pull toes upwards
Radial deviation	Bend wrist sideways by moving hand towards radius	**Feet**	
		Inversion	Turn the sole of foot inwards
Ulnar deviation	Bend wrist by moving hand sideways towards ulna	*Eversion*	Turn the sole of foot outwards
Fingers		**Toes**	
Flexion	Bend fingers towards palm	*Flexion*	Bend the toes towards the sole of the foot
Extension	Straighten fingers	*Extension*	Straighten the toes and bend upwards

just three to four seconds. You want a short duration to get a clear indication of any weakness. If you allow them to continue after this period they may apply sufficient mental determination to build up power in the muscle, matching the strength of the same muscle on the other side of the body – even if it is in fact weaker. The other problem that may arise is where the muscle you are testing is more powerful than the resistance you can offer from your arms. Again, if you allow too long for the muscle contraction you may be forced to move, and you will not be able to measure the resistance effectively.

When you begin testing, feel for differences in power to determine whether there is a weakness in a muscle. You will not have time to work your way around the whole body, so be selective and use the client history to determine which muscles you test. When you find an imbalance you will want to know why there is a weakness. Is the muscle damaged, or has it been in the past? Has the muscle atrophied, and if so, why? Is the muscle stronger because of the type of sport played, or because of some imbalance in your client's training programme? The answers to these questions are important in determining how you massage and what sort of exercises will be most beneficial.

Importantly, you need to recognise that it is often difficult to completely isolate and contract a single muscle. For example, if your client is lying prone on your couch and you ask them to flex the knee to 90 degrees so you can apply resistance to test the hamstrings, you need to remember that this contraction will involve all three muscles that make up the hamstrings – as well as other muscles that assist in the movement, such as the gastrocnemius, which also crosses the knee joint and acts to flex the knee. If they feel any discomfort in the region of the back of the knee, it may be that the heads of the gastrocnemius have been strained and the discomfort

or pain may prevent them from applying full power to the hamstrings. Different joint actions and sometimes different angles will help narrow down the options. In the example given you may start with the foot plantarflexed to reduce the amount of contraction available in the gatrocnemius, thereby allowing the hamstrings to contract in isolation.

The more you can learn about muscles and their actions, and the more you practise feeling for different muscles as they are working, the better your assessment will become. But be patient – this often takes plenty of practice and experience.

♦ Isolating a problem ♦

What are active, passive, and resisted movements?

These movements, described below, are a means of isolating problems. For example, if a person has impaired movement of a particular joint, you need to find out more about what is causing the joint dysfunction and whether massaging the soft tissues in the area is likely to alleviate the problem. If sports massage cannot help, the client may need to be referred to another specialist, such as an osteopath, physiotherapist, or even the nearest hospital. Sports massage may be appropriate *after* specialist treatment, to help relieve any remaining tension and restore flexibility so better joint and muscle function will be encouraged.

Active movements
Active movement is when a person moves a part of their body by their own effort (*see* Figure 7.5). Here, the client has been asked to flex their right knee, drawing the lower leg off the couch using predominantly the hamstring muscles.

71

Figure 7.5 Example of an active movement

Passive movements

Passive movement is when the therapist moves a part of a person's body for them (*see* Figure 7.6). By assisting the movement and performing a passive action the person is not using any muscle action; you are doing the work and the client's muscles should be relaxed. If the movement is impaired now, does it feel like a mechanical 'block' within the joint or is there a 'soft' feel at the present limit of the motion? Whichever it is, it is likely to be a joint problem which the sports massage therapist will not be trained or qualified to deal with.

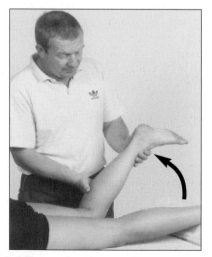

Figure 7.6 Example of a passive movement

Resisted movements

Resisted movement is when the person performs an active movement and while doing so, the therapist applies resistance to prevent it – in response, the person's muscles work to overcome the resistance. This is known as an *isometric contraction* (*see* Figure 7.7).

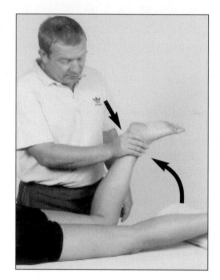

Figure 7.7 Example of a resisted movement

By resisting the movement and causing an isometric contraction, the muscles will work without movement between the articulating surfaces. If this causes discomfort or pain, it is likely to be caused by damaged or weakened muscle tissue or tendon. Sports massage will almost certainly help, but the timing of the massage will depend on how recently the problem arose. If it is an injury in the acute stage, sports massage should be delayed until the blood vessels heal (*see* Chapter 12, *Injury management*).

♦ Conclusions ♦

How much do I need to tell my client about what I find?

The answer is, very little. Few of us have perfect symmetry throughout the body, despite what we might think. If you highlight every minor imbalance, it may be psychologically damaging – particularly for those clients who are very sensitive about their physical condition. One of your tasks as a sports massage therapist is to motivate your client to adopt a balanced programme of exercise appropriate to their needs; therefore, telling them about every minor observation may prove counterproductive. Get to know your client before you decide on your approach.

After you have gathered all your findings, be selective about what you tell your client and make sure you keep a sense of perspective about each observation. Emphasise anything that has the potential to develop into something that may seriously impede their performance. If there is a minor problem that requires a little attention or modification in their training, then say so.

What if my observations do not match anything from my client's history?

Many people have imbalances that do not have a noticeable effect on the individual's daily life or sporting performance. Determining the cause may or may not be necessary: if there was no trauma that could have caused an imbalance, and no other obvious cause, it may be best left alone. What you need to ask yourself is: 'If my client is unaware of this and there are no side-effects, is it impairing their sporting performance and is it likely to harm them in the future?' If, in your opinion, the answer to these questions is: 'Unlikely', then it is best not to upset your client's routine. You may conclude that your client appears to have carried this imbalance for longer than they can remember and are coping with it without any ill-effects – or even awareness that there is a problem. If you intervene, you may create other problems that prove more detrimental. Worse still, they become aware of new physical stresses, which in the short term may impair their performance.

While there are many instances where you can encourage a client to slowly re-educate their body to correct posture and improve balance and performance, you must also accept that when the normal functioning of the body systems is disturbed, the body begins to adapt and compensate. This does not always result in side-effects that become a burden to the individual. The body may well adapt and continue functioning as well as before.

Are there any other factors that influence what I tell my client?

The other factor to consider is mental attitude: Does this client have the determination to see this programme through to its full conclusion? Will I see this client for treatments on a sufficiently regular basis to help them achieve these results? It takes time and effort to encourage soft tissues to readapt to stresses and to re-educate joints and muscles to function differently. To achieve results you will need your client's full co-operation in working through a programme of massage and correctional exercises. If the effects of the imbalance are not that noticeable, the person may not consider it important enough to persevere with the programme. It may take several sessions before you can judge your client's mental attitude and before they develop the necessary confidence in your programme.

Chapter 8

Developing touch and sense – palpation

♦ What is palpation? ♦

Palpation is the process of feeling and sensing the body through touch, and is used in sports massage to identify different body structures and their condition. It is therefore a *continuous* process, carried out as an integral part of massage with the mind constantly inter-preting and evaluating what the hands can feel. For this reason, palpation is dealt with here as a topic separate from the three main massage techniques described in the follow-ing chapter.

Although the foundation of this skill is based on knowledge, it must be developed through practice. To interpret what you feel and sense while you palpate the body, you must have a thorough knowledge of anatomy so that you can accurately identify the structures of the body under the surface of the skin. Chapter 3 discusses the the basics of anatomy for sports massage application. Surface anatomy, which is discussed later in this chapter, is used during palpation to guide the therapist to the areas of soft tissue that need to be assessed.

After identifying what you are feeling, your sensory powers are used to determine the physical state, texture and tension in the soft tissue. Any information gathered from your client's history, your visual and physical examinations, or from previous massage sessions will help you evaluate any abnormalities detected. Abnormalities in the

soft tissue may include scar tissue, muscle tears, fatty nodules or oedema; these are described below.

♦ How do you palpate? ♦

Since palpation is a sensory skill which should take place the whole time you are massaging, the entire palmar surfaces of the hands are used. However, to feel a small area, the pads of your fingers and thumbs are the best sensory areas of the hands and should be used extensively to assess the state of soft tissue. The amount of pressure needed depends on whether the problem lies in deep or superficial muscle tissue, and on how deeply you need to palpate. Very light movement over the surface is sometimes all that is necessary. If you can't palpate very deep tissue, you may be able to sense changes in the superficial layers as a guide. For example, a client may have a slight problem with a deep quadricep muscle such as vastus intermedius. You may not be able to feel this directly, but nevertheless detect an abnor-mally high amount of muscle tension in the surrounding muscles – including the over-lying rectus femoris muscle – resulting from the deeper problem.

When palpating, avoid using downward pressure through the thumb too frequently. The thumb joints are not designed to with-stand constant pressure of this kind and it may lead to aches and pain, which will hamper your skills and may even make massage uncomfortable for you. If you need to apply increased pressure, use the fingers of the other hand resting on the back of the first to add weight. (After you have palpated using finger and thumb pads, you can use the heel of the hand, which will allow you to apply much greater pressure with more ease.)

The area of the body you are palpating should be as relaxed as possible to maximise your sensory abilities. Movements should always be slow so that you can accurately identify the soft tissue; and any increase in pressure should be gradual to prevent discomfort to your client or tightening of the muscles. Always keep both hands in contact with the body, even if you are palpating with one hand only. The other hand may be used to sense light reflex actions in surrounding muscles.

The best way to palpate structures below the surface of the skin is to move the skin over the underlying tissue. Try this experiment to prove it to yourself: take an area with a clearly defined structure, such as the Achilles tendon, and – using a little oil – slide the pad of your thumb over the surface of the skin. Now hold the skin with the pad of the thumb and move the skin over the tendon. It is important that the part being massaged is adequately supported and stabilised by the other hand, so place your supporting hand (using the curve at the base of the your thumb) into the natural contour to the side of the Achilles tendon. This will prevent any lateral movement of the tendon itself. You'll find that the tendon feels more defined when you move the skin over the tendon, rather than the thumb over the skin.

Visible signs of inflammation indicate that an area may be tender or painful. Adjust the depth and pressure used to palpate these areas and encourage verbal feedback. Where possible, if an area is particularly tight and

harder to palpate, change the angle of a corresponding joint to shorten and relax the target muscles. For example, you may flex the knee to reduce the tension in the hamstring or calf muscles.

♦ What do soft tissue ♦ abnormalities feel like?

Always compare soft tissues. Some abnormalities are obvious, particularly if there are visible signs as explained earlier, and don't need further exploration; others need to be compared with surrounding muscles and with corresponding muscles on the opposite side of the body. Here are some examples of some common abnormalities.

♦ Where there is a *tear in the muscle,* you will usually feel a dip in its contour where the fibres have pulled apart. In severe cases the dip may actually be visible and permanent. In the early stages following a muscle tear injury, it may be difficult to feel because of possible swelling.

♦ *Scar tissue* usually results from a tear in the muscle. It will vary as to what it feels like, depending on how much time has passed since it was formed. Recent scar tissue has a fairly firm, compact feel to it, but gives a little as you apply pressure. Later, as it matures, it will become harder and eventually may feel as solid as bone tissue. The rate at which this takes place depends on several factors such as the individual's age and level of fitness; this is discussed in greater depth in Chapter 12, *Injury management.*

♦ *Fatty nodules* are sometimes situated on the under-surface of the skin. This produces a 'corrugated' feel when you perform a stroking movement over the surface of the skin.

◆ *Oedema* is where there is fluid in the soft tissue. This usually creates a soft, mobile feel to the tissue, so that as you palpate you can move the fluid around. However, if there is excessive fluid present then the skin can become tight, firmer and less mobile. At this stage touch may become uncomfortable or painful due to the increased pressure from the swelling on the sensory nerves.

◆ *Tension*. This may appear in many guises: while it may on many occasions be quite straightforward to detect tight muscles or whole groups of muscles, sometimes the tension may feel initially like the formation of scar tissue. Therapists often refer to these as 'knotted' areas. If the massage is effective in alleviating this tension you will soon detect much more pliable muscle.

◆ What if both sides of the ◆ body are abnormal?

This happens frequently. For example, both sets of hamstring muscles may be tight. In this case you need to compare the tissue with another part of the body. In the case of tight hamstrings you may use the quadriceps, which is the opposing muscle group, or the calves as a gauge of how tight the muscles are. While working, you may sense changes in these muscles from the previous massage session – caused perhaps by changes in training patterns and intensity, injury, poor stretching, and so on. So even after the initial history-taking, it is important when sensing these changes to get verbal feedback from the client as to what the causes might be.

◆ How do I improve my ◆ palpation skills?

Practice and experience

There is no substitute for practice. Being able to compare what you are feeling with the many different tissues you have felt in the past is the most effective way of improving your skills. Practice and experience allow you to make faster and more accurate judgements as you palpate, and raise your skill level and reputation as a sports massage therapist. However, gaining practical experience takes time, but while you are doing so, there are other ways in which you can improve your skills. These are detailed below.

Improve the strength and dexterity of your hands and forearms

By improving the strength and dexterity of your hands and forearms you will be able to palpate for longer without fatiguing. Your sensory skills will also become more acute. There are various exercisers that you can use to develop strength and dexterity, such as handgrips, putty or 'stress balls'. Alternatively, substitute objects, such as a tennis ball, can help just as well. For example, you can improve strength by squeezing a tennis ball with the whole hand and then just with the fingertips. Dexterity can be improved by devising games such as trying to move the ball between finger and thumb tips around the hand (palm upwards), using no more than three at a time. As you improve, try changing direction, speeding up, using the other hand – and then both hands at once!

Improve your sensory powers

To improve your sensory powers, practise feeling the surface of objects without any visual contact. For example, place a coin under a number of pages of a book and try to feel the pattern on its surface. As your senses are heightened, try the same exercise with a different coin under more pages this time. Alternatively, place intricately shaped objects under a cloth and then try to feel each part in detail through the cloth.

♦ Surface anatomy ♦

What is surface anatomy?

This is a term commonly used in sports science, referring to the bony prominences or areas of bone that can be seen or felt just beneath the surface of the skin. These form surface 'landmarks' that provide a guide to finding soft tissues such as muscles, tendons and ligaments. Sports massage therapists must be able to identify surface landmarks to understand which tissues are being palpated.

How do I identify the surface landmarks?

First, you need to have a thorough knowledge and understanding of the skeletal system (*see* Chapter 3, pp. 15–21 for reference). As well as being able to identify each bone, you need to know how they articulate and which bones are more prominent during certain movements. Second, you need to know each muscle, and their origins and insertions. It is easier to learn muscle origins and insertions by learning muscle actions. They will make much more sense when you understand where the points of attachment are – and how, by drawing these together, muscle contraction brings about joint action and movement.

Use Figures 8.1 and 8.2 to help you practise locating some of the surface landmarks of the body. You can also use Figure 3.4 of the skeletal system in Chapter 3 for reference. When you have worked through the figures and checked your answers with those given on p. 78, practise locating some landmarks on yourself and other people. You will find that structures do vary slightly from one person to the next.

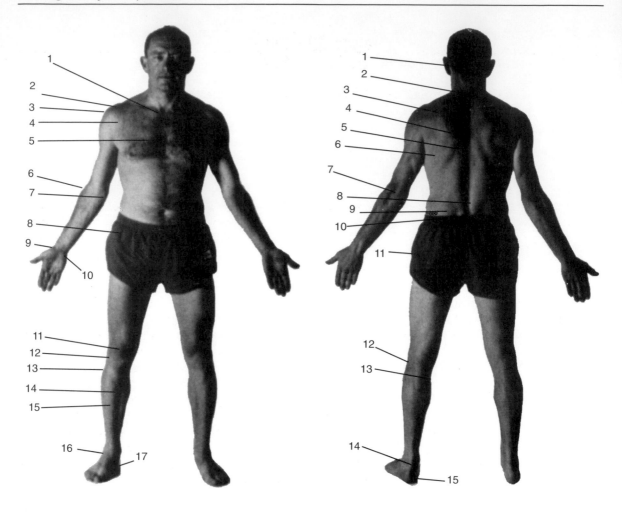

Figure 8.1 Identifying some of the surface landmarks of the body – anterior view

Figure 8.2 Identifying some of the surface landmarks of the body – posterior view

1. Sternoclavicular joint 2. Acromium process 3. Head of humerus 4. Coracoid process 5. Sternum 6. Lateral epicondyle 7. Medial epicondyle 8. Anterior superior iliac spine 9. Radial styloid process 10. Ulnar styloid process 11. Patella 12. Tibial plateau 13. Head of fibula 14. Tibial tubercle 15. Tibia 16. Lateral malleolus (distal end of fibula) 17. Medial malleolus (distal end of tibia)

1. Occipital hollow 2. Spinous process of C7 3. Spine of scapula 4. Medial border of scapula 5. Spinous processes of thoracic vertebrae 6. Inferior angle of scapula 7. Olecranon process 8. Lumbar vertebrae 9. Posterior superior iliac spine 10. Sacrum 11. Greater trochanter of femur 12. Lateral femoral condyle 13. Medial femoral condyle 14. Achilles tendon 15. Calcaneum

Chapter 9

How to massage – the techniques

This chapter describes the various techniques of sports massage, showing how the palpatory skills discussed in Chapter 8 can be incorporated. It also considers factors influencing the effective application of sports massage techniques, such as the therapist's posture, the position of the hands for each technique, and performing the correct movement to derive maximum benefit for the client. For information about equipment, *see* Chapter 2, and Appendix 1.

You must be physically and mentally fit for all massage sessions. If you are unwell, under stress or physically tired your efforts will not produce the same results and your client will notice. A healthy mental state allows you to put aside any thoughts or problems of your own so you can focus on your client. You must not massage if you are feeling unwell, since you may expose your client to infection.

Giving massage is very therapeutic, and once you begin a session it becomes easy to focus your attention on your client. Maintaining your fitness for massage, particularly for extended periods, requires the right equipment (*see* p. 76), posture, and techniques.

♦ Posture ♦

It is vital that you maintain good posture throughout every massage session. Your ability to focus and give a good massage to every client will depend on maintaining

maximum comfort. The correct posture will also delay the onset of fatigue, particularly during long working periods. Limited facilities for pre-competition massage may prohibit the use of a couch, and massaging may become uncomfortable or tiring in such circumstances.

Assuming you have an appropriate massage couch, the following guidelines on posture should be adhered to in every massage session. Ignoring these principles will increase the stress on specific joints and muscle groups – and *you* may end up seeking the services of a sports massage therapist, yourself!

First, work with your back reasonably straight rather than bent over. By flexing the hips and knees, instead of your back, you will be able to achieve good posture, movement and pressure. The position of your feet also has an important bearing on long-term comfort. As an example, consider the position of the feet when massaging the back of a leg (*see* Figure 9.1). If you position both of your feet at one end of the couch you may have to stretch to reach the upper part of the limb, causing discomfort in your lumbar region. Instead, move one foot round to the side of the couch. Keep your knees bent to give you the comfort and flexibility needed to massage the leg thoroughly and to maintain even pressure throughout each movement. From this position, move through your knees and hips so that your upper body remains upright and comfortable. Finally, whenever possible, keep your arms and hands fully relaxed and

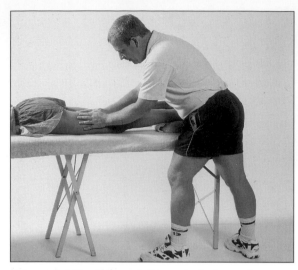

Figure 9.1 Position of therapist's feet when massaging the back of the leg

allow them to do the work without over-straining or wasting your much-needed energy. The hands should conform with the natural contours of the client's body.

♦ The techniques ♦ – some general points

There are three main techniques used in general sports massage therapy:

♦ Effleurage
♦ Petrissage
♦ Frictions

Other specialised techniques often used in massage include passive stretches, and some of these are described later in this chapter. Massage effleurage and petrissage techniques direct pressure towards the heart to increase venous and lymphatic flow. This also ensures that no undue pressure of blood causes any

damage to closed valves. Valves exist in veins to prevent backflow of blood. Blood being forced through the blood vessels under normal pressure – by the heart, and to a lesser extent muscular activity – pushes the valves situated in the veins open. As the pressure subsides and the blood moves back, this forces the valves to shut and stops the blood flowing back any further. Therefore, any sustained pressure brought about by stroking movements in massage should be in the same direction as normal venous bloodflow (i.e. towards the heart) to prevent increasing the pressure on, and risking damage to, the valves. Some effleurage and petrissage techniques may also be adapted to use short strokes to stretch muscle fibres. Because the strokes are short there is no risk of excessive pressure causing damage to the valves.

Before discussing each sports massage technique in detail, we will first look at some general techniques relevant to massage practice.

What areas of the hand do I use?

The most important areas used in sports massage are the palm of the hand, the palmar surfaces of the fingers and thumbs, and the pads of the fingers and thumbs. Figure 9.2 illustrates the position of these areas on the hand.

These surfaces are the most sensitive areas used in massage, providing sensory feedback so that you can palpate the tissue and control the pressure. This is a vital skill for the sports massage therapist, who relies on information about the tissue being massaged at any given moment in order to know how to adjust the pressure and timing of the massage to benefit the client. For these reasons, bony surfaces, such as knuckles and elbows, should not be used for general sports massage.

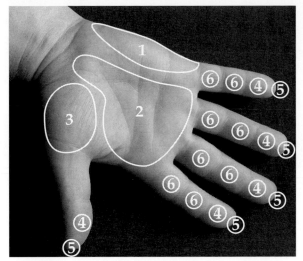

Figure 9.2 The areas of the hand used in sports massage

Key:
1. Ulnar border
2. Palmar surface
3. Base of thumb
4. Pads of fingers and thumb
5. Tips of fingers and thumb
6. Palmar surface of fingers and thumb

Should I always maintain contact with my client?

You should maintain contact with your client whenever possible. This reassures the client and helps them to relax, particularly when they are lying face down and cannot see you. If you lose contact they may begin to wonder whether you have finished and if they should move. By keeping a hand resting on their skin they know the massage is still in progress. In most instances it is quite easy to maintain contact when you are picking up the oil or moving round to the other side of the couch. Even when applying more oil you can simply turn the hand over that is in contact with the client, pour oil on to the palm of the hand, rub the oil between your hands and then turn the hand to face down again.

At competitions, sports massage is often performed in tents, changing rooms and so on, with plenty of other people about. Conditions are not always ideal, so if you are not able to keep all your towels, oils, tissues, etc. near to you, don't worry about maintaining contact – it helps, but it is not vital. If you do break contact and leave your client, make sure you cover them and do not leave them exposed.

How do I apply the oil?

Always place the oil on your hands, not directly on to the client. Try to warm it between your hands whenever possible. If this is not feasible, warn your client – it may be that no matter how hard you try, the only thing that will warm your hands is the first massage and your first client.

♦ Effleurage ♦

What is effleurage?

The word effleurage derives from the French word, *effleurer*, which means 'to skim'. It is a form of massage involving stroking movements with the hands sliding over the skin, and is always used at the beginning and end of – as well as in between other techniques during – a massage session. The stroking technique of effleurage may be used with varying pressure and speed according to the purpose and stage of the massage. Effleurage includes light stroking, firm stroking and deep stroking

How to do effleurage

The basis of effleurage is stroking with light to firm pressure, using a wide surface area of the palm of the hand and fingers. Pressure is sustained throughout the stroke and the direction of the stroke is always towards the heart to encourage venous return (*see* p. 80). This is opposed to the technique of petrissage (*see* p. 83), where the stroke direction – while still always being directed towards the heart, is from proximal to distal. When you use strokes which pass over any bony prominences you must ease off the pressure – since there is no benefit to massaging over bone, and it may be uncomfortable for the client – but still maintain contact. The movements may be performed using both hands simultaneously or by alternating hands. On the return stroke, the hands maintain light contact and avoid the path taken on the upward stroke. The position and direction of the movements will vary according to the technique and part of the body you are working on. For example, long stroking movements may be performed up the leg, whereas the movements may be more circular on the back – *see* Chapter 10 for further detail.

Effleurage should be carried out in a smooth, rhythmical and relaxed manner, starting with a light touch at the start of a session and building up to deeper pressure with slower movements for increased circulation and stretching of the tissues later. The hands must be relaxed and follow the natural contours of the client's body. The technique should not be rushed – you need time to identify and focus on any abnormalities in the tissue that may require further attention later in the session. Quick movements will not help the client relax, and if a tender area is missed it will almost certainly be more painful if discovered later when using deeper techniques such as petrissage!

Specific effleurage techniques appropriate for each area of the body are discussed and illustrated in detail in the next chapter.

What does effleurage achieve?

The aims of effleurage are to:

♦ introduce touch to the client;
♦ put the client at ease;
♦ warm the superficial tissues;
♦ relax the muscles;
♦ allow the therapist to palpate and sense the condition of the tissue;
♦ stimulate the peripheral nerves (*see* also Chapter 5, p. 52);
♦ increase lymph and blood flow, and thus aid the removal of waste products;
♦ stretch tissues;
♦ relax a client before the end of the massage.

Not all of these aims may necessarily be achieved at once. The speed with which each technique is applied in relation to the circumstances will determine what you are aiming for. For example, lighter, brisk movements will be designed to stimulate and energise your client before exercise or competition while the same techniques applied more slowly after exercise may be aimed at helping the removal of waste products and relaxation.

It is essential, however, to achieve your aims using effleurage before moving on to deeper techniques. If the muscles have not relaxed sufficiently, deep tissue massage may be uncomfortable and even detrimental to the client. The more pliable the superficial tissue, the greater the opportunity for the massage to have an effect on the deep muscles.

To complete any massage, use light effleurage to relax the client, particularly if intense – and possibly even painful – movements have been used beforehand.

◆ Petrissage ◆

What is petrissage?

Petrissage comes from the French word, *pétrir*, which means 'to knead'. The basic petrissage movement is to compress and then release the soft tissue, using either direct pressure or by picking up and squeezing the skin and muscle.

Petrissage is generally used to have a deeper effect on soft tissue than effleurage, and includes kneading, squeezing, picking up, shaking (and other techniques described as wringing and rolling, which achieve much the same results).

How to do petrissage

As with effleurage, the part of the technique applying pressure is usually directed towards the heart to encourage venous return. The surface of the therapist's hands often remain in almost static contact with the client's skin while moving it over the underlying muscle.

However, with petrissage the overall direction is from proximal to distal (*see* p. 13), as opposed to effleurage, where the stroke and overall direction are both towards the heart. To achieve this, the therapist first applies generally shorter strokes (towards the heart), but after one or more strokes deliberately slides the hands distally before commencing the technique again. The aim of this is to push blood out of an area of soft tissue by applying pressure, then releasing the pressure before repeating the manoeuvre distally to force fresh blood and nutrients into the area just 'vacated'.

What does petrissage achieve?

The aims of petrissage are to:

◆ increase mobility between tissue interfaces;
◆ stretch muscle fibres;
◆ aid the interchange of tissue fluids (*see* above);
◆ increase venous and lymphatic return;
◆ relax muscles;
◆ aid the removal of waste products.

Since petrissage techniques are specifically applied to and have an effect upon deeper tissue, they are both ineffective and difficult to perform on narrow parts of the limbs. Therefore, you must pay particular attention – as with all massage techniques – to the purpose of the massage when using petrissage.

◆ Frictions ◆

What are frictions?

Frictions are small movements over isolated areas using the pads of the fingers or thumbs – using considerable pressure compared to the techniques described so far. The pads of your fingers or thumbs move with your client's skin in either a circular or transverse direction, and may be used on muscles, tendons and ligaments. As explained in Chapter 8 (*see* pp. 74–5), finger and thumb pads can be used with medium to firm pressure for exploratory purposes – to feel small areas under the surface. Greater pressure is used for deeper and sometimes more painful movements aimed at separating muscle fibres and breaking down recent scar tissue.

The therapist's finger or thumb pads must remain in static contact with the skin, moving the subcutaneous tissue over the deeper

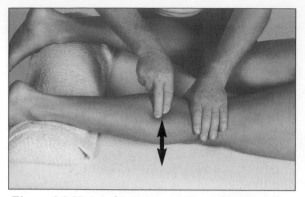

Figure 9.3 Using frictions on the calf muscles. The arrows show the fingers moving side to side across the direction of the muscle fibre.

tissue. Figure 9.3 shows frictions being performed on the calf muscles – *see* also Chapter 10, p. 109 for frictions on the feet.

How to do frictions

When performing frictions for the purpose of separating muscle fibres and breaking down scar tissue, the client must be warned that these procedures may be painful or at the very least uncomfortable, although the pain will subside after a short while. This is an advanced massage technique and should only be used with when you are confident that:

♦ you can accurately locate a lesion (an injury or altered structure);
♦ you know how to place the affected tissue on full stretch – i.e. you are fully aware of where the origins and insertions are located;
♦ you are confident that there will be an overall benefit.

To be successful in treating lesions, frictions should be repeated during massage two to three times a week. The purpose is to deliberately break down tissue, stimulate

vaso-dilation (widening of the blood vessels), increase localised circulation, and restore *elasticity*.

Particular attention must be paid to how long and how vigorously frictions are applied. Applying frictions for a period of several minutes during a massage session to a very confined area is quite normal. Using frictions for longer can have a particularly detrimental effect by irritating or even damaging healthy muscle fibres and causing inflammation. It is far better to err on the side of caution and increase the amount of frictions applied during a subsequent massage session if necessary.

What do frictions do?

The aims of frictions are to:

♦ separate adhesions between fibres;
♦ break down scar tissues;
♦ restore elasticity;
♦ stimulate vaso-dilation and blood flow;
♦ stimulate the healing process;
♦ realign new scar tissue.

♦ Other sport massage ♦ techniques

Tapotement describes techniques such as *hacking* and *cupping* which have their place in massage aimed towards relaxation. Hacking (*see* Figure 9.4) is a technique in which both hands alternately strike the skin with the lateral borders of the fifth finger of each hand. As the other fingers close together on striking the skin, a characteristic sound is made. It is known to stimulate the skin and superficial muscle tissue, preparing the muscle for exercise and hence being an option for pre-competition massage. Cupping involves making an air-tight concave shape with the hand so that, as it strikes the surface, the air caught underneath is compressed, creating a vibration that penetrates the tissues. Characteristically, it also creates a vacuum as the hands are pulled away, and therefore by stimulating the superficial tissue can move blood away from deep tissue, a fact which may be considered counterproductive for sports massage. Other techniques achieve most of the same effects, together with additional benefits, more efficiently so tapotement is not widely used.

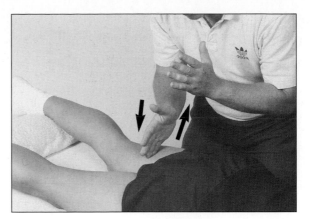

Figure 9.4 Tapotement – hacking

Chapter 10

How to massage – practical application

This chapter describes how to prepare for massage and how to massage each part of the body. There is no set order to the various parts of the body, but the techniques described for each are in a logical sequence, enabling you to provide effective, thorough and comfortable massage. It is up to you to decide with your client which areas of the body are to be massaged, placing them in order according to the needs of the client and how easy it is to progress from one area to the next.

The particular techniques used are the most appropriate ones for each specific area of the body, and are presented in their most logical sequence for each part – working from lighter to deeper, more pressured movements in each case. However, always remember to repeat the lighter effleurage techniques at the end of each sequence to relax your client.

Advice is given on how to stand, the position of the hands, and how to start and finish each movement, with additional tips to help. This chapter should be used as a reference until you remember the movements and can perform them in a relaxed and rhythmical manner.

♦ How do I prepare my ♦ client for massage?

In Chapter 7, the client assessment, including history-taking and the physical examination, were discussed in detail. Once the assessment is finished, and you have explained briefly to your client what you intend to achieve from the massage, direct them on what garments to remove and how to position themselves on the couch. Give confident, relaxed and clear instructions so that your client will not feel embarrassed. Always respect your client's privacy when they are undressing, whatever the surroundings in which you are working. If you are in a treatment room and you do not have a screen, it may be tactful for you to turn away or to leave the room while they prepare. If you are at a sporting event and there are other people in the massage area, screen the client by holding up a large towel.

For sports massage, as a general rule, it is only necessary to undress down to under-wear. The use of towels is illustrated in the following photographs of the massage techniques. It is important to be familiar with the use of towels, as it is appropriate in many sporting environments to keep otherwise uncovered areas of the body warm while massaging the exposed areas. Other reasons for the use of towels are described below.

Positioning the client on the couch

The couch roll or rolled bath towel should be positioned on the couch beneath the knees or ankles, depending on whether you have asked the client to lie prone or supine (*see* Figure 10.1). Once they are on the couch, make sure that the supports are in the right positions. Place another bath towel over the body and ask whether the client is comfortable. Draw back the towel and expose the area you are about to massage. If appropriate, the towel can be tucked under the edge of the client's clothing. This achieves two things: first, it protects their clothes from the oil; and second, it clearly defines the boundary of the area you are about to massage. This is particularly reassuring for clients of the opposite sex. If, for example, you are about to massage the back of one leg, draw the towel away to expose the leg and position the feet apart so that there is room between the legs for your hand to massage without making contact with the other leg. Tuck the towel under the bottom of the client's shorts or pants. If you do not do this and your fingertips pass underneath the edge of the towel, your client may feel uneasy because there is no guide to 'tell' them the limit of the area of your massage.

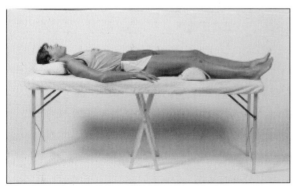

Figure 10.1 Position of the client on the couch (supine), with supports under the neck and knees

◆ The massage ◆ – some general tips

How do I start?

First, remember the points discussed in Chapter 9:

◆ Pay particular attention to the position of your feet and your posture.
◆ Try and maintain contact with your client at all times.
◆ Always place the oil on the hands first.
◆ Think about the purpose of each technique as you massage.

Begin by massaging your client using effleurage (*see* pp. 81–2) to introduce them to the feeling of your hands and to the movements and the pressure. Movements should be smooth and rhythmical and the pressure should be comfortable – neither too light nor too heavy, sufficient to sense a change. The pace should be steady, but not too slow; you must move the hands briskly enough to stimulate the circulation, but not so quickly that the person feels disturbed by the speed of your hands. Focus on relaxing the client mentally and physically, and at the same time concentrate your attention on the state of the soft tissue you are massaging. Once this is achieved, you can begin to palpate for any areas of tension or tenderness, or any abnormalities.

During the massage

After the initial stage of the massage, check that the client is comfortable with the pressure. Ask them to tell you at any point if they feel anything such as soreness, tightness, pain, etc. during the session. Although you will develop sensory skills through the use of your hands, good massage always relies on constant verbal feedback from your client. No matter how experienced you become, you cannot possibly know what your client feels – nor should you judge the amount of pressure they may like by an assessment of their body size or muscle bulk. While you may expect someone who has plenty of muscle to like firm pressure, they may prefer a lighter massage. Conversely, there are many small-framed, lean people who enjoy very firm pressure. When you ask your client, 'Is this pressure comfortable for you?' most will respond with an almost automatic response of: 'Yes that's fine', without even thinking about it. So give them another opportunity to say just how much pressure they really like by asking, 'Would you prefer it any lighter or firmer?'

♦ How to massage ♦ – using this section

As explained in the introduction to this chapter, the following descriptions cover the main massage techniques as appropriate, applied to each part of the body in turn. The order in which the parts of the body are presented is intended as a guide only; the sports massage therapist and client together will best judge which area(s) require the most attention.

Advice on how to massage each part of the body is preceded by a 'preparation' section. As a general rule, you will prepare your client for massage as discussed earlier in this chapter, on p. 86–7 – so this text is intended to highlight any additional tips which may be specific to the particular area of the body that is being described. For example, when massaging the back of a female client, you will need to undo her bra strap – letting her know what you are doing beforehand.

The section on preparation is followed by advice on the therapist's 'starting position'. This includes both body position – for example, to one side of and facing the couch, adjacent to the client's lumbar region – and the initial position of the hands before the technique begins. It should be noted that massage of each part of the body is a continuous process, involving smooth transition from one technique to another (for example, for the back – light followed by firm effleurage; petrissage; then firm effleurage once again, and so on). For this reason, and to avoid repetition, the text will then only indicate when *changes* in the therapist's body and hand position should occur, once the initial positioning has been described.

Finally, the techniques are described step by step, as teaching points in bullet-point form. Sub-headings are numbered to indicate the number of times variations on each type of massage occur – and the amount of pressure required. For example, 'Effleurage (ii): firm stroking' refers to the second time the therapist applies the technique of effleurage to a particular area of the body, this time exerting a firm pressure.

◆ Posterior massage ◆

Back massage

Eighty per cent of the population will experience back problems at some point of their lives. For more details of the common symptoms please refer to p. 94.

Figure 10.2

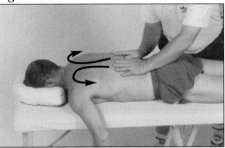

(a)

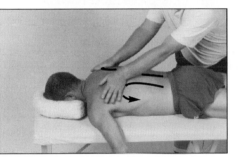

(b)

Preparation
When massaging a female client who is wearing a bra, advise her that you need to undo the bra to massage her back – *before* doing so! And always re-fasten the strap when you have finished.

Starting position
Stand adjacent to your client's waist with your feet angled towards the head of the couch, and your body turned so that you can place your hands on each side of the lumbar spine with the fingers pointing to the head.

Effleurage (i): light stroking (Figure 10.2)
◆ Begin your strokes in the direction indicated in Fig. 10.2(a), maintaining an even pressure throughout the palmar surfaces of the hands and fingers.
◆ Each movement will fan outwards at a point further up the back (Fig. 10.2(b)) before sweeping back down the sides to the start with a light touch.
◆ Continue the movement until you reach the shoulders and then begin again with small movements just fanning outwards, gradually making larger movements as the massage progresses up the back.
◆ Finish after the whole back has been covered, and when you feel the skin warming and becoming more supple.

Figure 10.3

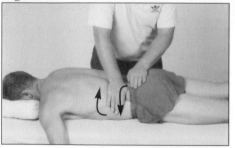

(a)

(b)

Effleurage (ii): firm stroking (Figure 10.3)

♦ *Starting position*: moving your feet and body, turn to face the lumbar region. Put your hands side by side – fingers facing away from you – with one resting over the sacrum.

♦ Use the other hand to apply firm strokes away from you over the far side of the lower lumbar region (Fig. 10.3(a)). The whole of the hand remains in full contact with the skin, with the pressure finishing through the heel of the hand.

♦ If you feel the pelvic rim as you stroke, adjust the pressure of the hand so only the area proximal to the pelvic rim receives pressure.

♦ Then, keeping one hand in place on the sacrum, turn the other inwards so that your fingers are facing you and apply similar strokes to the side of the lower lumber region nearest to you, as in Fig. 10.3(b). Keep your elbow raised.

Figure 10.4

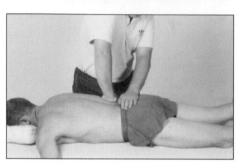

(a)

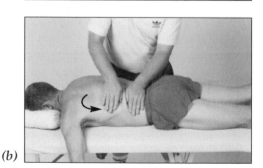

(b)

Petrissage (i): firm kneading (Figure 10.4)

♦ *Starting position*: move your feet and body to face the mid-back region and rest your hands on the far side of the back.

♦ While keeping one hand still to act as an anchor, move the other in a circle, 'picking up' and squeezing the superficial tissue as the border of one thumb glides past the other towards you, as in Fig. 10.4(a).

♦ It is important to perform this action with the circling hand moving towards you during the squeezing phase; this avoids the danger of picking up and scratching the skin with the ends of the thumb and fingers. If you feel you have picked up sufficient tissue and applied the correct pressure, glide the hand past without pinching or causing any discomfort to the client, as in Fig. 10.4(b).

♦ Once you have completed the circle, slide the hand acting as the anchor up an inch or so and circle the other hand towards it again.

♦ Repeat the procedure all the way up the back. Continue over the scapula if there is enough soft tissue to pick up. (*Continued over page.*)

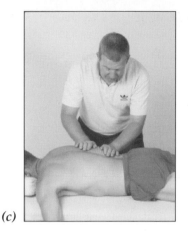

(c)

♦ Slide your hands back to the lumbar region and start again on a section nearer to the spine.

♦ The next time, slide your hands down to a starting point on the side near you and divide this into two further sections for massage.

♦ With practice, you will become better at judging how much pressure to use between the hands to pick up and squeeze. If at any time the tissue creases, ease off the pressure and continue gliding past the other hand.

Figure 10.5

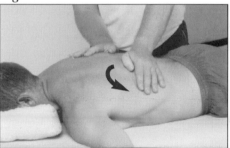

Effleurage (iii): firm stroking (Figure 10.5)

♦ *Starting position*: return to the original position (*see* Fig. 10.2(a) above) with your feet facing and angled towards the head of the couch.

♦ Place your hands in the same starting position for the first effleurage stroke, on either side of the spine.

♦ This time, massage with one hand only, starting on the far side. Use the heel of the hand to circle away from the spine using short, much firmer strokes, as in Fig. 10.5. Although the whole hand remains in contact with the skin, the pressure is applied through the heel of the hand across the fibres of the erector spinae muscles.

♦ The other hand rests on the surface of the other side of the spine and may be used to sense any changes in other back muscles while you are massaging. It is best to use only one hand when you increase the pressure so you can focus your attention on a confined area. Continue this manoeuvre up the side of the spine until you reach the scapula and continue as below.

♦ Repeat, working up the nearside of the spine.

Effleurage (iv): firm stroking

♦ Once you reach the scapula, ease the heel of the hand over the medial border of the scapula without any pressure before re-applying pressure with a very short stroke to compress the muscles over the back of the scapula.

91

♦ By positioning your shoulder girdles over the client's lumbar region, you will be able to complete the same manoeuvres to the nearside of the spine without having to move to the other side of the couch.

Effleurage (v): deep stroking (Figure 10.6)

Figure 10.6

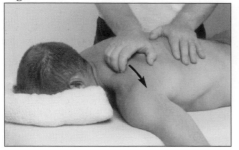

♦ *Starting position*: all the previous strokes have been applied using the left hand to the left side of the spine and the right hand to the right side. In this movement you may find it easier to use the opposite hand to massage, with the other hand resting on the lateral aspect of the shoulder.
♦ Flex the fingers of your massaging hand so that you can tuck the pads of four fingers into the hollow above the scapula, as in Fig. 10.6. This hollow is created by the superior fossa of the scapula where the fibres of the supraspinatus lie.
♦ Apply short, firm strokes over this muscle away from the spine and towards the shoulder. If you feel any fibrous material or areas of tension you may wish to change the movement to small circular actions to ease any tensions from the muscle.
♦ Change hands and repeat on the opposite side.

Petrissage (ii): picking up – medium pressure (Figure 10.7)

Figure 10.7

♦ *Starting position*: stand adjacent to midway up your client's back and angled towards their head.
♦ Apply light to firm movements to the upper fibres of trapezius on both sides by grasping the muscle between the thumb and forefingers of each hand, as in Fig. 10.7.
♦ While keeping the fingers reasonably straight, lift, squeeze and allow the soft tissues to slide out of your grasp in one movement.

Figure 10.8

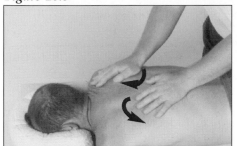

(a)

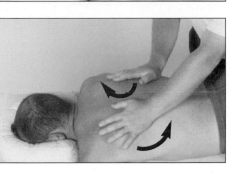

(b)

Petrissage (iii) – medium pressure (Figure 10.8)

♦ *Starting position:* place your hands either side of the spine on the upper back, with your fingers facing the client's head.

♦ Circle each hand alternately, applying medium to firm pressure as you are moving away from the spine, as in Fig. 10.8(a). At the same time slowly slide the hands down the back. As one hand is pushing out exerting pressure, the other should be gliding round the lower part of a circle to maintain contact, as in Fig. 10.8(b).

Figure 10.9

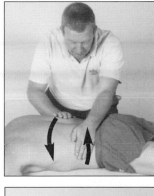

(a)

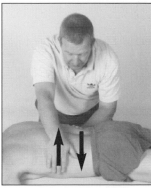

(b)

Effleurage (vi): 'Kangaroo stretch' – medium to firm pressure (Figure 10.9)

♦ *Starting position:* stand with feet and body facing the side of the couch, starting with the hands either side of the torso and just above the pelvic rim.

♦ With firm pressure, pull one hand across the back and at the same time push the other hand to the opposite side, as in Fig. 10.9(a). You will need to bend your knees to position yourself so that you can apply sufficient pressure to make this really invigorating for your client.

♦ Keep the hands on pathways at least an inch apart so that if you manage to pick up any superficial tissue you will not pinch the client as the hands cross the spine.

♦ There is no need to ease off the pressure as you pass over the spine; there should not be any downward pressure exerted as the action is one of pulling and pushing the soft tissues over the spine.

Back problems

Symptoms of back problems are:

♦ localised pain to the spine;
♦ loss of feeling or tingling sensations (pins and needles) in any part of the limbs, which may indicate spinal nerve impingement.

If the client has either or both of these symptoms you need to check thoroughly for any spine-related problems before massage. You can check for problems by:

♦ observing the client's gait, posture and symmetry while standing and walking (*see* Fig. 7.2, p. 67);
♦ checking and comparing mobility and range of motion of joints (*see* p. 68);
♦ palpating on the side of each vertebrae and applying firm pressure while the client is lying prone to check for any muscle spasm or undue tension.

If the client reports any different sensations in any part of the body while you are palpating, this may indicate a nerve impingement or an irritation emanating from the spine. In these cases, sports massage is contraindicated and the client should be referred to an appropriate specialist. If, after checking, the symptoms appear mild, sports massage may be used to relax the muscles in the back region (*see* Figures 10.2–10.9 for appropriate massage techniques). However, the client should still be referred to appropriate specialist help if any back problem is evident.

Neck massage

Preparation
When massaging the neck it is important to place the head facing downwards so that the neck muscles are neither on stretch or too shortened. This is made easier with the use of a facehole in the couch which allows your client to remain comfortable and breathe easily. Instruct your client to get into this position before you start.

Starting position
Stand adjacent to midway up your client's back, with your feet and body angled towards their head.

Figure 10.10

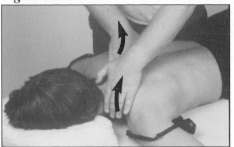

(a)

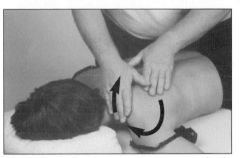

(b)

Effleurage (i): light stroking (Figure 10.10)

♦ Place one hand with the palm into the crook of the neck and stroke the neck muscles towards you with a firm stroking movement, as in Fig. 10.10(a).

♦ As the hand slides over the ridge of muscle release the pressure and circle round to repeat the movement At the same time, place the other hand in the starting position, ready to carry out a similar stroke, as in Fig. 10.10(b).

♦ Continue the movement with alternate hands: one hand maintains contact while the other releases, producing a continuous stroking and stretching of the muscles.

Figure 10.11

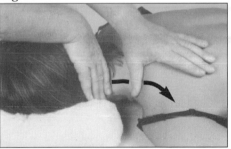

Effleurage (ii): deep stroking (Figure 10.11)

♦ *Starting position:* move round and stand at the head of the couch.

♦ Hold the neck with one hand and place the lateral border of the thumb just laterally to the lower neck.

♦ Stroke over the upper fibres of the trapezius. By pushing the thumb firmly away from the other hand a deep stretch may be applied.

Figure 10.12

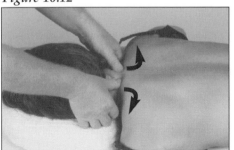

Effleurage (iii): deep stroking (Figure 10.12)

♦ Standing at the head of the couch, place the thumbs on the back of the neck.

♦ Using the thumbs, perform small circular actions either side of the cervical spine to loosen and stretch the soft tissue. The pressure should be increased on the upward and outward part of the circle, and glide round to the start position.

Gluteals massage

Preparation

Massage of this area may be important for many sportspeople because the gluteals are powerful muscles that are used in most sporting actions. The deeper muscles – known as the *piriformis* group of muscles – that externally rotate the femur will also benefit from massage to this area. You may need to explain these benefits to the client beforehand, as they may be embarrassed about exposing this area for massage.

The most discreet way of exposing the gluteals depends on what your client is wearing. If they are wearing running-style shorts that are loose-fitting and made of relatively lightweight material, it is easy to draw up the shorts on one side towards the belt-line. If the shorts are made of heavy material and are tight-fitting, first ensure the person is covered with a towel and then lift the top of the towel slightly, so your client can draw the shorts down before replacing the towel. Draw the towel from one side to the midline and secure the towel by placing one hand on the towel and sacrum.

Starting position

Stand with your feet facing and adjacent to the middle of the couch.

Figure 10.13

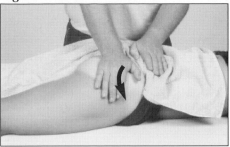

Effleurage (i): light to increasing pressure (Figure 10.13)

♦ Massage the gluteals on the far side using strokes moving from the midline and in the direction of the muscle fibres. Even if you are massaging someone of the opposite sex, this method will not be too intrusive.

♦ The pressure should be directed through the heel of the hand and may deepen progressively as the muscles become more relaxed. You will gradually begin to sense the resistance of the underlying tissues, including the piriformis group of external rotator muscles. At this point follow the next manoeuvre.

Figure 10.14

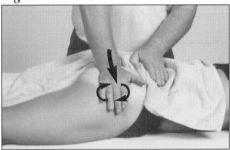

Petrissage (i): kneading – firm pressure (Figure 10.14)

♦ Alter the above technique by 'holding' the superficial tissues with the heel of your hand, maintaining firm pressure and performing small circular movements.

♦ By not sliding your hand over the skin you can move the superficial tissue over deeper structures to massage them.

Figure 10.15

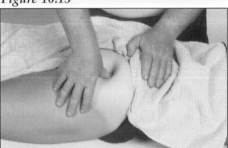

Petrissage (ii): kneading – firm pressure (Figure 10.15)

♦ *Starting position:* still keeping one hand over the sacrum, place the pad of the other thumb over the piriformis group that you have already sensed above.

♦ Using the thumb, apply more direct and firmer pressure to the deeper muscles. As before, hold the skin so that there is no sliding over the surface. Very small circular movements will allow you to use the superficial muscle to massage over the deeper tissue.

Figure 10.16

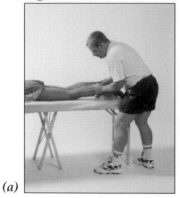

(a)

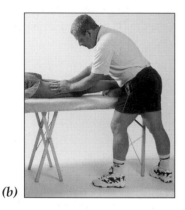

(b)

Leg massage (posterior)

Preparation

Stand with one foot angled round and to the rear of the back leg of the couch. The other foot should be alongside the couch with the toes angled more towards the head of the couch. This will allow you to bend the joints in your lower limbs to move your upper body and prevent you from stretching as you massage up the back of your client's leg.

Starting position

Position your hands on the lower part of the calf, with fingers and thumbs pointing towards the gluteals.

Effleurage (i): light stroking (Figure 10.16)

♦ Begin a stroking action, applying pressure all the way up the back of the leg, but easing off over the back of the knee.
♦ Finish by sweeping the hands out to the sides of the limb and quickly back down the limb to the starting position. Maintain contact throughout the movement.

Figure 10.17

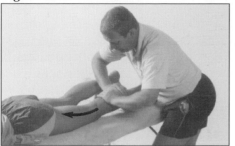

(a)

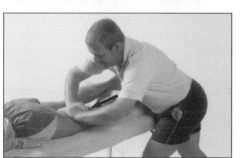

(b)

Effleurage (ii): 'carpenter's plane' – light stroking (Figure 10.17)

♦ *Starting position*: with your feet in the same position as above, lower your upper body so that when you start the stroke the pressure is directed more *up* the limb rather than compressing downwards.

♦ Wrap each hand around the girth of the leg, with the fingers of both hands pointing towards the sides of the leg and both ulnar surfaces of the hands facing up the limb, as in Fig. 10.17(a).

♦ With the hands relaxed around the limb, but not overlapping, commence a firm stroking action moving proximally, reducing the pressure to a light touch over the back of the knee, as in Fig. 10.17(b).

♦ As the girth of the limb increases, draw your wrists further to the sides of the limb – so maintaining contact with most of the exposed surface.

Figure 10.18

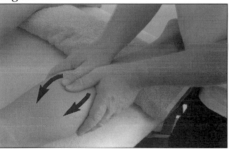

Effleurage (iii): light stroking (Figure 10.18)

♦ *Starting position:* keep your feet in the same position as above, but assume a more upright position.

♦ Start with your hands resting on the lower calf, with the thumbs on the top of the soleus muscle and their medial borders touching. The rest of the hand faces forwards and is cupped around the limb.

♦ Maintain this position of the hands, moving them up the calf as far as the back of the knee. The thumbs should be kept on a level plane so that they divide the two lobes of the gastrocnemius muscle.

♦ Focus your attention on the stroking action of the palms of the hands. Remember that this is still a form of effleurage, so there should be no downward pressure into the calf from the thumbs.

Petrissage for the legs

Used on the legs, petrissage requires co-ordination, rhythm and plenty of practice to be performed properly and to be effective. Four types of petrissage are described: three applied with the pressure longitudinally, and the fourth performed from the side in a transverse direction. With each manoeuvre, do not be too concerned about how much soft tissue you pick up; this is not important as it is the pressure phase that brings about the effective part of the massage. Remember, the overall direction must be proximal to distal, regardless of which way the pressure of each movement is applied. All of these petrissage techniques are applied to the bulkier muscle areas of the calves and hamstrings.

Figure 10.19

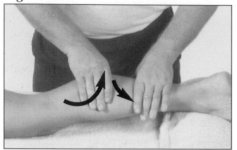

(a)

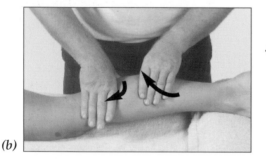

(b)

Petrissage (i): squeezing – light pressure (Figure 10.19)

♦ *Starting position:* stand facing the limb from the side of the couch. Use each hand alternately to pick up and squeeze an area of the calf muscles, as in Fig. 10.19(a).
♦ After squeezing, release and allow the skin to slide from your grasp so the other hand can repeat the process on the same surface area, as in Fig. 10.19(b).
♦ As you continue, you should achieve a pleasant, rhythmical action that is very effective in raising the surface temperature of the tissue and increasing circulation. Once started, both hands can work down the limb.
♦ This is a particularly useful technique to use for pre-competition massage. Done at a quicker pace it will stimulate and prepare the athlete for action.

Figure 10.20

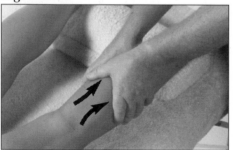

(a)

Petrissage (ii): kneading – firm pressure (Figure 10.20)

♦ *Starting position:* stand alongside the couch, with your feet angled towards the head so that your body tends to do the same.
♦ This petrissage technique for the legs involves spreading the thumb and fingers of one hand around the girth of the limb, and then placing the other in a similar fashion over the top, so that the hands work in a singular action together.
♦ Using both hands, lift and draw the tissue up and towards you, maintaining full static contact between the client's skin and your hands, as in Fig. 10.20(a). To do this you must ensure that most of the oil has already been absorbed into the skin during effleurage.

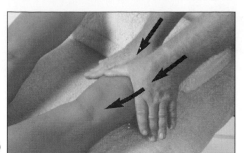

(b)

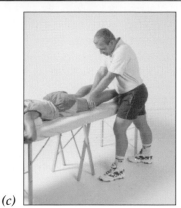

(c)

♦ Allow your hands to spread in a fan-like fashion, releasing the skin as you do but maintaining contact using the surface between your thumb and index finger, as in Fig. 10.20(b).

♦ Holding the same area of skin, compress and push the soft tissue up the limb. Do not allow your hands to slide over the surface.

♦ As you finish pushing, release the pressure and return the hands back to the starting position by closing the fingers lightly around the limb to commence the movement again.

♦ After massaging an area of muscle, allow your hands to slide down the limb an inch or so to work a new area.

♦ The amount of pressure you apply will be directly related to the amount of effort exerted from your arms. If you or your client requires greater pressure, you may simply straighten your arms and use your upper body weight to increase the compression of the muscle under your hands, as shown in Fig. 10.20(c). Be aware of the angle of your arms to ensure that you are not compressing the muscle against bone.

Figure 10.21

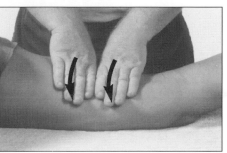

(a)

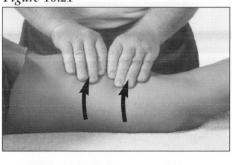

(b)

Petrissage (iii) – medium pressure (Figure 10.21)

♦ *Starting position:* stand and face the feet, with your body towards the leg from the side of the couch.

♦ This third technique works in a transverse direction across the muscle fibres and incorporates two basic movements.

♦ Commence with the hands together, thumbs positioned as anchors on the nearside of the limb.

♦ Lightly contour round the limb, as in Fig. 10.21(a), using a light grasp to draw the muscle and skin towards you (as described in petrissage (ii) above).

♦ Straighten the fingers and roll the straightened fingers away from you, as in Fig. 10.21(b). This movement rolls the superficial tissues over the underlying tissues, mobilising fluids and stretching the fibres in the deep muscle.

Figure 10.22

(a)

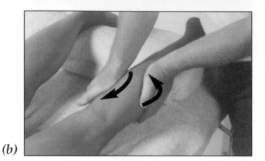

(b)

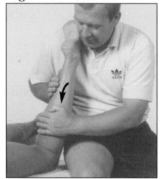

Figure 10.23

(a)

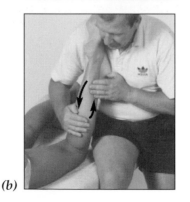

(b)

Petrissage (iv): circular kneading – firm pressure (Figure 10.22)

♦ *Starting position:* stand alongside the couch, with your feet angled towards the head so that your body tends to do the same.

♦ Place the heel of each hand on top of the calf with the fingers facing downwards.

♦ Slide each hand proximally and outwards, exerting pressure through the heel of the hand, as in Fig. 10.22(a).

♦ As the hand finishes the downward part of the stroke, the hand sweeps round with light contact, forming a circle back to the starting position, as in Fig. 10.22(b).

♦ Each hand alternates so the pressure is first to one side of the limb, then the other. At the same time as the hands are circling up the limb, they are gradually sliding distally.

♦ Slide back to the top of the section you are working on and repeat.

Technique tips: If your client has particularly tight calves or hamstrings, try flexing the knee and supporting the lower limb, as shown in Fig. 10.23. Muscles that have been taken off stretch are easier to work with stroking movements to help relax them.

◆ Anterior massage ◆

Preparing for massage: turning the client over

Figure 10.24

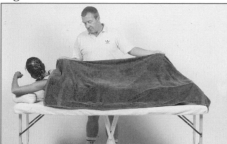

(a)

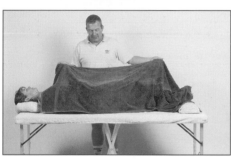

(b)

Turning the client over should be done with the minimum of confusion. Advise your client to prepare to turn over, and ask them to lift their head so that you can put a towel or small pillow there ready. If your client is in a state of undress and you need to keep them covered, use the procedure illustrated in Figure 10.24:

◆ Ask your client to turn their head to face you, as in Fig. 10.24(a).
◆ Lift the nearside edge of the towel up and hold it just above the level of the client's body.
◆ Ask them to turn onto their back, moving in the direction they are facing. They will now turn, pulling against the towel and keeping it taught – so remaining covered, as in Fig. 10.24(b).
◆ Once the client has turned over, rest the towel back down.
◆ Ask them to lift their legs while you move the support bolster from the ankle region to the underside of the knees.

Upper leg massage (anterior) – Figures 10.25–10.30

Figure 10.25 (see Figure 10.16(a))

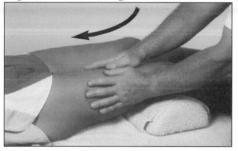

Figure 10.26 (see Figure 10.16(b))

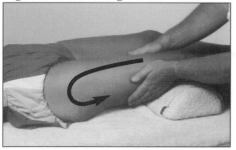

The techniques, which may be applied to the front of the thighs, are similar to those used for the posterior legs – including the first stroking movement with the fingers facing up the limb, and all the petrissage movements except the 'carpenter's plane' (Fig. 10.1). Petrissage movements must be applied with some caution to the anterior of the thighs, because the rectus femoris usually feels tight over the femur. Too much pressure over this midline will be uncomfortable for your client. Refer to the figure numbers shown in brackers for the corresponding posterior leg massage.

Figure 10.27 (see Figure 10.20(a))

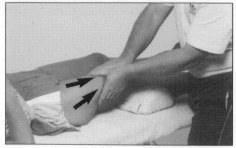

Figure 10.28 (see Figure 10.20(b))

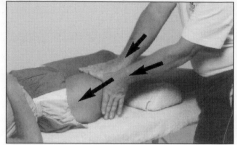

Figure 10.29 (see Figure 10.22(a))

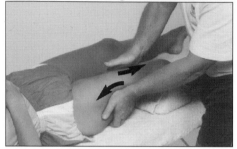

Figure 10.30 (see Figure 10.22(b))

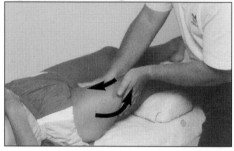

Lower leg massage (anterior)

Figure 10.31

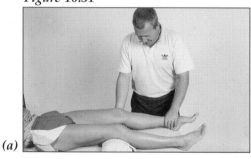

(a)

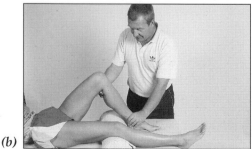

(b)

Preparation (Figure 10.31)

The surface of the tibia is prominent around the front part of the lower leg, so there are only few areas of the lower leg that can be massaged successfully. To massage the soft tissue you must first move the leg into a suitable position:

♦ Ask your client to relax while you place one hand under the knee and grasp the front of the ankle with the other hand, as in Fig. 10.31(a).
♦ Lift under the knee until it is flexed to 90 degrees, moving the ankle towards the client's body at the same time, as in Fig. 10.31(b).

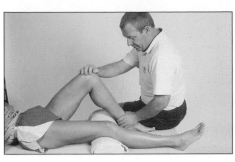

(c)

Starting position
- Sit on the couch next to the edge of your client's foot (as in Fig. 10.31(c), without putting any of your body-weight on the foot, telling your client as you do so. This seated position steadies the leg so their foot will not slip forwards and both of your hands are free to work.
- When you finish massaging the lower limb, return your hands to the same position at the knee and ankle to support the leg. Ease yourself off the couch, and extend the client's leg back to its original position.
- With the fingers of both hands, feel the ridge of the tibia, which is slightly medial to the midline of the anterior aspect of the leg. Lateral to this you will feel the belly of the anterior tibialis.

Figure 10.32

Petrissage (i): kneading – medium to firm pressure (Figure 10.32)
- Starting below the knee, massage the anterior tibialis using circular strokes, with your elbow elevated so that you are pushing at 45 degrees to the bone.
- The pressure is applied at the top part of the circle as you move away from the midline.
- The circles should be small enough so they move the skin over the anterior tibialis and compress the muscle over the surface of the tibia.
- Each circle moves lower down the limb before returning to the starting position. Increase the intensity as you repeat the movement down the leg.

Figure 10.33

Petrissage (ii): kneading – medium to firm pressure (Figure 10.33)
- Support the leg at the knee with one hand, and with the other hand curl all four finger tips round the edge of the tibia a short distance above the ankle.
- Gently push until you can feel more resistance than normal. This resistance comes from the muscles contained in the posterior compartment. How deeply this resistance is felt will vary between individuals.
- Once the posterior compartment is located, hold the fibres with the tips of the fingers and stretch the muscle away from the bone with very small circular actions. Your fingers will need to stay in contact with the tibia as you work this muscle, otherwise you will loose contact with the muscle itself.

♦ Each circular movement progresses up the limb until you no longer feel resistance – this is where the muscle 'disappears' behind the tibia to its origin.

♦ You will often find small nodules and bumps on this muscle which may be tender for your client so be ready to ease off the pressure when necessary. For the same reasons, make sure your actions are slow and deliberate so that you can feel for these areas and react quickly.

Chest massage

Preparation
The chest does not often require massage for sport, but there are times – particularly when someone has been using weight machines to strengthen the pectoral muscles – when this needs to be done. For female clients you will obviously need to work above the line of their bra or a towel covering them.

Figure 10.34

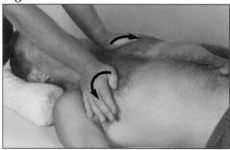

Starting position
Stand at the head of the couch facing your client.

Effleurage (i): light to medium stroking (Figure 10.34)
♦ Start by resting the heels of your hands either side of the sternum with your fingers facing outwards.
♦ Use the hand resting on the chest to apply stroking movements. The pressure is through the heel of the hand and away from the sternum. This is a steady, controlled, stroking action which only increases in pressure with each stroke according to the depth of muscle tissue present.

Figure 10.35

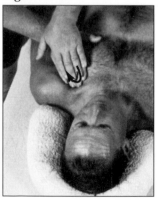

Effleurage (ii): deep stroking – medium pressure (Figure 10.35)
♦ *Starting position:* now work from the side of the couch, with your feet positioned in line with your body towards the head of the couch.
♦ Apply small, circular actions with the pads of your fingers to the muscle attachments below the clavicle. This area is normally sensitive, so although you may apply firm pressure, do so with care and a steady, controlled movement.

Figure 10.36

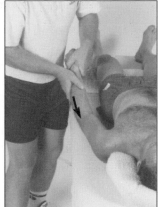

(a)

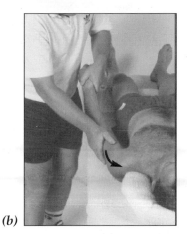

(b)

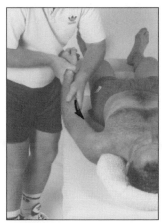

(c)

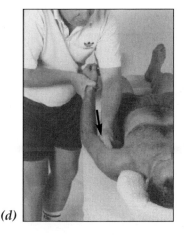

(d)

Arm massage

Preparation
The supine position is the easiest position from which to massage the arms because your client will be more disposed to relaxing them. The techniques described in this section are the same as those described later in the section with the client seated (*see* 'Pre-competition massage' p. 114).

Starting position
Stand adjacent to your client's waist facing towards the head with your feet angled in the same direction.

Effleurage (i) – light stroking (Figure 10.36)
♦ Gently lift the arm by the wrist with one hand and shake it lightly to promote relaxation, as in Fig. 10.36(a); some people find it difficult to 'let go' of the arm.
♦ Still holding the wrist, use the palm of the other hand to apply effleurage strokes towards the shoulder to the lateral aspect of the arm and over the deltoid, as in Fig. 10.36(b).
♦ Apply similar strokes to the medial aspect of the arm by swapping hands. With each manoeuvre keep the upper arm raised off the couch so that your hand encircles the limb, as in Fig. 10.36(c) and (d).

Figure 10.37

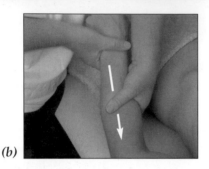

(a)

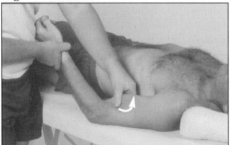

(b)

Effleurage (ii) – firm stroking (Figure 10.37)

♦ Flex the client's elbow and rest it on the couch so you are looking down at the forearm.
♦ Hold the client's wrist with one hand, and use the flat surfaces of the thumb and middle finger of the other hand to apply a *box squeeze* to the extensors and flexors of the forearm. A box squeeze is a single stroke up the arm with firm pressure, as shown in Fig. 10.37(a).
♦ If the girth of the arm is too great to cover from one side only, you may change hands and apply the same stroke from the other side (Fig. 10.37(b)). Make sure in both instances that you are working the soft tissue and not the bony prominences of the radius and ulnar.

Figure 10.38

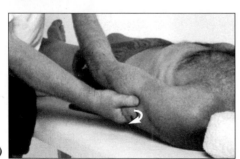

(a)

(b)

Petrissage: kneading – medium pressure (Figure 10.38)

♦ *Starting position:* standing by your client's waist with your feet in the same position, lift the arm by holding the wrist with one hand.
♦ With the other hand, use the thumb and fingers to apply a kneading action to the biceps by picking up, squeezing and releasing the skin, as in Fig. 10.38(a).
♦ Work your way up the belly of the muscle before repeating the movement from the starting position.
♦ Change hands and use the same technique on the triceps, as in Fig. 10.38(b).

Foot massage

Preparation

Before massaging the feet, always check for sensitive areas, abnormalities, blisters, veruccaes (warts), and possible infections such as athlete's foot. When massaging the feet you need to apply firm pressure, so it can be hard work. Consider how much punishment your feet take in everyday activities and you will begin to appreciate that the muscles, tendons, and ligaments must be very tough and require a certain amount of pressure to have any effect during massage.

Starting position

Position your client so that the edge of their heels are level with one end of the couch. Stand to the side and beyond the end of the foot of the couch.

Effleurage (i) – firm stroking (Figure 10.39)

♦ Place one hand over the dorsal aspect of the foot and place the heel of the other hand on the ball of the foot, as in Fig. 10.39(a).
♦ Move each hand simultaneously in the same direction – the upper hand applying strokes to the dorsal aspect, and the heel of the other hand applying much firmer pressure to the plantar surface, as in Fig. 10.39(b). To do this, your elbow must be level with your hand.
♦ The pressure on the plantar surface is applied to the soft tissue between the ball of the foot and the heel.

Figure 10.39

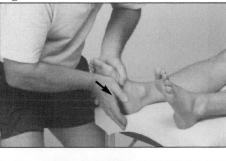

(a)

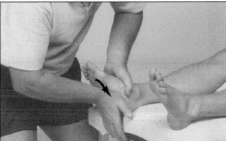

(b)

Figure 10.40

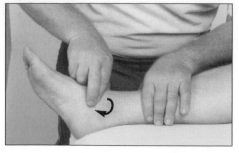

Frictions – medium pressure (Figure 10.40)

♦ *Starting position:* stand with your feet positioned so that you are closer to your client.
♦ Hold the leg with one hand and position the other with pads of fingers or thumb resting on the area to be massaged.
♦ Use small circular frictions with the pads of the fingers and thumbs to work the tendons and ligaments around the ankles.
♦ You will need to have a good knowledge of the anatomy of the foot, as there are a lot of bony structures, some tendons and ligaments and very little muscle tissue. You must also adjust the pressure applied accordingly.

Figure 10.41

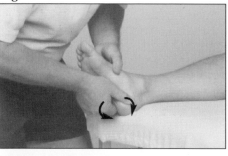

(a)

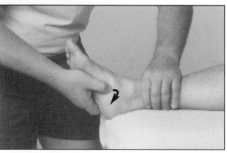

(b)

Petrissage (i): kneading – firm pressure (Figure 10.41)

♦ *Starting position:* start in the same position, but hold the middle of the dorsal aspect of the foot with one hand.
♦ Grasp the heel pad between the borders of your thumb and forefinger and apply alternating squeezing movements to the sides of the heel pad, as in Fig. 10.41(a).
♦ Use the thumb to work the soft tissue of the arch of the foot, as in Fig. 10.41(b).

Figure 10.42

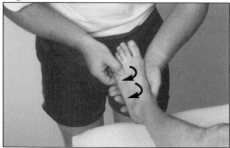

Petrissage (ii): kneading – medium pressure (Figure 10.42)

♦ *Starting position:* stand at the end of the couch.
♦ Apply light circular movements with the pad of your thumb between the tendons on the dorsal aspect of the foot, working from the toes towards the leg.

Figure 10.43

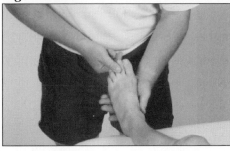

Stretching toes – firm pressure (Figure 10.43)

♦ Gently hold each toe between the pad of your thumb and the border of our index finger, and stretch them by squeezing and pulling.

Figure 10.44

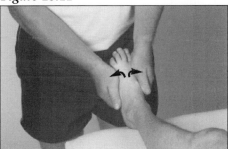

'Kit-Kat stretch' – firm pressure (Figure 10.44)

This technique provides a comfortable massage for your client and it gives an invigorating stretch of the feet.

♦ *Starting position:* stand beyond the end of the couch.
♦ Hold the foot with both hands, with the heels of your hands on the dorsal surface. Be careful not to push your fingernails into the sole of the foot.
♦ Slide the hands outwards, applying firm pressure – as though you are trying to 'break open' the foot.

♦ Ilio tibial band release ♦

The ilio tibial band (ITB) is different from all the other muscles in the body and requires a special treatment in sports massage called the *ilio tibial band release*. The ITB consists of a long, tendon-like band of tough tissue running up the lateral aspect of the leg between the knee and the greater trochanter of the femur. It joins the belly of the tensor facia latae. The ITB has a strong influence over gait and provides support for the knee. If the ITB is overused and becomes tight, it can have a detrimental effect on gait and the knee. The ITB release, as the name implies, releases the tension and your client will feel the difference as soon as they begin to walk, often reporting that the legs feel 'lighter'. The ITB release should always be used on both legs to ensure that your client's gait is balanced.

While most sports massage techniques are relaxing and comfortable, the ITB release may be uncomfortable or even painful. It is therefore important to understand what effects it has and when it is appropriate, or not, to use it.

When is it appropriate to use the ITB release?

Consider using the ITB release when:

♦ your client complains of knee pain or tightness to the outer part of the thighs;
♦ your client's history reveals either a rigorous programme or a recent increase in training.

(Remember, the amount of training is relative to what is normal for your client, so don't necessarily preclude anyone who is not training six days a week.)

Preparing your client for the ITB release

Once you decide your client may benefit from the ITB release you should explain to them why you suggest using this technique and what is involved. Your verbal instructions, for example, may be as follows:

There is an area here called the ilio tibial band or ITB which feels very tight. I think you will benefit from a technique called the ilio tibial band release; unfortunately, this is likely to be very uncomfortable. (Allow your client to signal their agreement at this point, perhaps with 'okay' or simply nodding.) When I say so, I'd like you to take a deep breath in, and again when I say so, breathe out slowly. As you exhale I will apply very firm pressure here. I will do this only once to this leg. Is that clear?

Starting position

Stand with your feet astride and your toes facing the head of the couch.

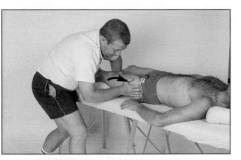

Figure 10.45

(a)

(b)

How to do the ITB release (Figure 10.45)

♦ Carefully palpate along the line of the ITB (this will feel like a particularly tight band, above which lies the bulk of vastus lateralis muscle).

♦ Position yourself as above, with one hand on the medial part of the leg above the knee, and the elbow out to prevent the other leg lifting. (Sometimes the level of pain is quite a shock and the client may react by trying to sit up.)

♦ Place the heel of the other hand on the ITB just above the lateral aspect of the knee with the fingers facing up the limb. Your elbow should be positioned at an angle of about 70 degrees so you can apply maximum pressure, as in Fig. 10.45(a). (Do not position it at a right-angle, or you will simply compress the tissue directly on to the bone.)

♦ Keep your knees bent and your feet in the 'stance' position – you need to be able to move the whole of your upper body to maintain constant pressure as the heel of your hand slides up the leg as in Fig. 10.45(b).

♦ When your fingers reach the greater trochanter of the femur, ease off the pressure so the heel of your hand doesn't press on this bony prominence.

♦ The ITB release lasts about four to five seconds and should be applied with extreme pressure as your client breathes out. Watch your hands, not your client's face, as you move, and as soon as you finish return to light effleurage (*see* Figs. 10.25 and 10.26 on p. 103).

When should you be cautious about releasing the ITB?

There are two main reasons for being cautious:

1 Do not use it close to a competition: your client may need time to adapt to the different feeling in their gait (depending on how perceptive and sensitive they are to their own performance).

2. Do not use it too often: remember, tight ITBs are caused by overuse and this takes time. If a client returns a week after you used the ITB release and says they are still experiencing problems with their knees or ITBs, there must be another cause. In this case, you may refer your client to a physiotherapist or osteopath to check their skeletal alignment and possible cause of the problem.

After the massage is over you will need to advise your client on what may have caused the problem, and how to stretch the ITB to help prevent the problem occurring again. Stretches for the ITB are described in Chapter 11, p. 137, Figure 11.11.

♦ After the massage ♦

Tell your client you have finished and to relax for a couple of minutes before sitting up. Then ask the client to remain sitting for a few minutes to allow their body to adjust to being upright – they may feel dizzy for a few moments after lying down for some time. Then tell them to dress and join you when they are ready to discuss your findings, recommendations and the next appointment. (For guidelines on the post-massage discussion, refer to Chapter 7, pp. 64–5. Chapter 11 also provides details on post-massage care for your client, including stretching exercises.) Finally, as clients sometimes feel thirsty after massage, keep fresh drinking water available in your treatment area.

♦ Pre-competition massage ♦

The sports massage therapist has to adapt quickly to all types of situations and may often be required to work without a couch and in a very limited time period. The main aims of pre-competition massage are:

♦ to boost the circulation rapidly and increase blood flow;
♦ to warm the area;
♦ to relax the muscles;
♦ by stimulating circulation increase the supply of nutrients and oxygen to the muscles to stimulate the athlete mentally.

Pre-competition massage is performed briskly, using sufficient oil to prevent any discomfort to the athlete. However, the initial movements should still be performed slowly to allow you time to assess the state of the soft tissue. If the athlete is tense you should continue slow movements while encouraging the athlete to relax. If, as you would expect from someone about to compete, the athlete is injury-free and they are not tense, quicken the movements to provide maximum stimulation. You will always find some athletes that are particularly tense or anxious before the 'big event' who will need calming down.

While you may use some squeezing and kneading techniques during this brief massage, it is vital that these are not applied deeply or for too long. Such movements could fatigue the athlete or induce a deep state of relaxation that is inappropriate for a pre-competition massage.

In pre-competition massage you apply a few strokes to a particular area and then move to another part – for example, the front of the thigh and then the back of the thigh. This is to ensure that all areas are kept warm and you avoid any discomfort from staying in one position for too long.

♦ How to massage a seated client ♦

The neck, shoulders, arms and legs can be massaged with your client seated in a chair. Massaging with the client in a chair is not as effective as using a couch because the muscles will tense to maintain posture. This tension needs to be reduced to a minimum. The correct positions for these massages are detailed below.

Neck and shoulder massage (seated)

Figure 10.46

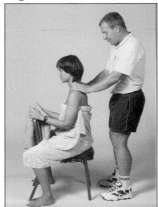

Preparation (Figure 10.46)
Ask your client to sit astride the chair, facing the back of it with the hands holding on. This position keeps the postural muscles, such as the erectae spinae in the back, relaxed. It also allows the client to use their arms to support themselves as you apply pressure.

Starting position
Stand behind your client with your feet apart to steady yourself.

Figure 10.47

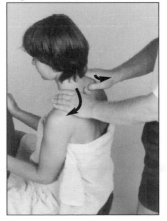

Effleurage (i) – medium stroking (Figure 10.47)
♦ Using the palms and fingers of both hands, apply simultaneous stroking movements from the hairline down over the deltoid muscles of the shoulders. Most of the pressure is exerted through the medial borders of the base of the index fingers. The thumbs are merely positioned as a guide and do not actually massage.
♦ Once you have passed the deltoids (and reach the upper arm), sweep round and back to the starting position. Increase the pressure with each movement and as the tissue warms.

Figure 10.48

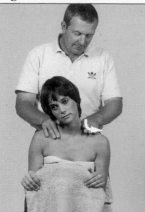

Effleurage (ii): firm stroking (Figure 10.48)

♦ *Starting position:* place one hand on the upper fibres of the trapezius muscle. Ask your client to tilt their head towards your hand and extend your index finger until it rests on the side of the client's jaw bone. Your hand should not be supporting any weight; it is providing a guide for your client.
♦ With the other hand, stroke downwards over the stretched upper fibres of the trapezius muscle, applying firm pressure through the medial border of the index finger, but maintaining contact through the whole of the palmar surface of the hand.
♦ Change the position of the hands and the client's head and repeat to the other side.

Figure 10.49

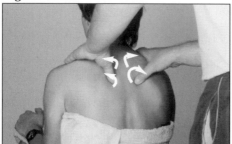

Effleurage (iii): firm stroking (Figure 10.49)

This massages the rhomboids area between the spine and the medial borders of the scapulae. The superior border of the scapulae is particularly prone to tension and may require more attention.

♦ Place the fingers of each hand over the trapezius muscle and reach as far down the shoulders as you can with your thumbs.
♦ Apply circular movements with the thumbs, applying the pressure during the movement away from the spine.
♦ Allow the thumbs to slide gradually upwards until you reach the superior border of the scapulae.
♦ Do not be tempted to go too deep, too soon: too much pressure may irritate already sensitive tissue and can be counterproductive. Be patient and wait for results.

Figure 10.50

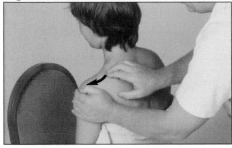

Effleurage (iv): deep stroking (Figure 10.50)

This massages the supraspinatus, which is one of the rotator cuff muscles.

♦ *Starting position:* lower your upper body so that you can angle your wrist and fingers as described below.

♦ Support the side of the left shoulder with the palm of your left hand and tuck the ends of your fingers of the right hand into the superior fossa of the left scapula. If you have difficulty locating the superior fossa, first find the spine (ridge) of the scapula and feel just above this.

♦ Stroke the skin with the right hand, moving towards the supporting left hand and applying firm pressure. You are now massaging over the supraspinatus. Increase the pressure gradually with each stroke.

♦ Change hands and apply the same technique to the other side.

Figure 10.51

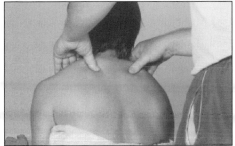

Petrissage: kneading (Figure 10.51)

♦ *Starting position:* rest your hands on the upper fibres of trapezius as though your are about to 'lift'.

♦ Use the fingers and thumbs of both hands simultaneously to pick up the upper trapezius.

♦ Squeeze and allow the skin to slide from your grasp.

Figure 10.52

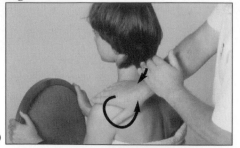

(a)

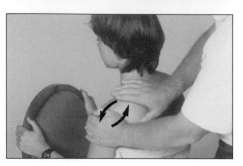

(b)

Effleurage (v): firm stroking (Figure 10.52)

♦ *Starting position:* with the palmar surface of one hand resting above the upper part of their shoulder.
♦ Use both hands independently to apply firm strokes over the deltoid from the neck downwards: one hand remains in contact and sweeps round to the starting position; the other lifts off and alternates with the first, as in Fig. 10.52(b).
♦ Apply the same technique to the other side.

Arm massage (seated)

Preparation

The hardest part about massaging the arms when the client is seated is keeping the arm relaxed. The client will often try and help by unwittingly holding the arm at an angle from the shoulder. It is best to keep the arm hanging by the side, where it will be in a relaxed position. Keep a towel on the client's lap so if you need to put the arm down at any stage the oil will not get on the client's clothes.

Starting position

Make yourself comfortable using a towel or cushion to kneel by the side of your client.

Figure 10.53

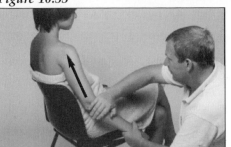

(a)

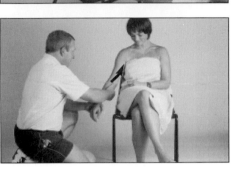

(b)

Effleurage (i) – light stroking (Figure 10.53)

♦ Hold the arm around the wrist with one hand. Apply effleurage strokes with the palm of the other hand, encircling the lateral aspect of the arm.

♦ Work from the wrist upwards with the ulnar surface of your hand leading. Stroke all the way up the arm and over the deltoid, as in Fig. 10.53(a).

♦ Using the same hand, stroke the medial aspect of the arm with the radial surface of your hand leading, as in Fig. 10.53(b).

Figure 10.54

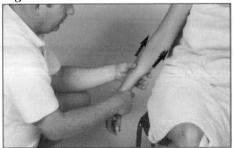

Effleurage (ii): firm stroking (Figure 10.54)

♦ *Starting position:* as above, but hold your client by the wrist and keep the arm in the relaxed position.

♦ Use the flat surfaces of the thumb and middle finger to apply a box squeeze to the extensors and flexors of the forearm (*see* also Fig. 10.37, p. 108).

Figure 10.55

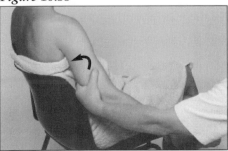

Petrissage: kneading – firm pressure (Figure 10.55)

♦ *Starting position:* draw your client's wrist and arm upwards, making it easier for you to gain access to the upper arm.

♦ Use the thumbs and fingers to apply a kneading action to the triceps by picking up, squeezing and releasing them and working your way towards the shoulder.

♦ Change hands and use the same technique for the biceps.

Figure 10.56

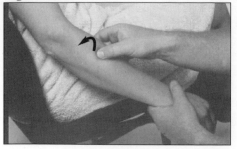

Effleurage (iii): deep stroking (Figure 10.56)

♦ *Starting position:* kneeling by your client's side, hold the arm by the wrist with one hand and massage with the other.
♦ Using the pad of your thumb, apply circular movements to work the tendons of the flexors and extensors of the forearm.

Leg massage (seated)

Figure 10.57

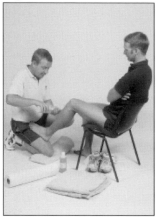

Preparation

Figure 10.57 shows how to perform pre-competition leg massage seated, i.e. without the use of a couch. This may prove uncomfortable for you, but you will not need to spend too long in one position.

Starting position

To start, kneel on one leg with one foot on the floor. This will allow you to move forwards later if you need to raise their leg – *see* hamstring massage below. Place the client's foot on your thigh and move forwards so the client's knee is flexed to approximately 90 degrees. From this position you should be able to reach all surfaces of the leg.

Figure 10.58

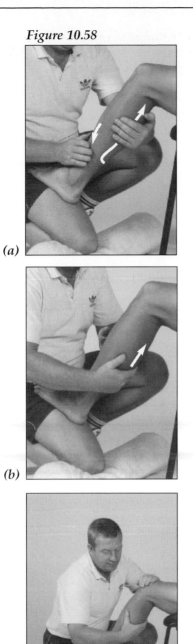

(a)

(b)

(c)

Effleurage (i) – light stroking (Figure 10.58)

♦ Reach round to the back of the limb and stroke the calf muscle proximally, alternating the hands. As one hand is applying pressure up the back of the limb, the other is moving lightly down the side to the starting position, as in Figs. 10.58(a) and (b).

♦ Begin slowly and check the state of the muscles. If they are not tense, increase the pace, making the movements brisk.

♦ If the leg becomes unsteady, place one hand on the knee and use the other hand to massage, as in Fig. 10.58(c).

Figure 10.59

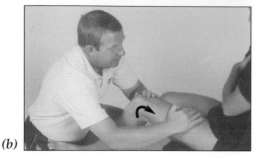

(a)

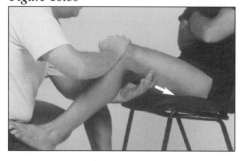

(b)

Effleurage (ii) – light stroking (Figure 10.59)

This technique is for the quadriceps.

♦ *Starting position:* place the palmar surfaces of each hand on the top of the thigh above the knee, one just above the other

♦ Stroke up the leg, leading with the ulnar border of the hand. Repeat the same movement using the other hand.

♦ As each hand finishes the stroke at the top of the leg, sweep back along the side of the leg to the starting position, maintaining contact at all times.

Figure 10.60

Effleurage (iii) – firm stroking (Figure 10.60)

This technique is for the hamstrings. It uses firm pressure and you need to keep one hand on the knee to steady the limb.

♦ *Starting position:* use the outside hand to hold the knee, since the client will tend to relax with the knee in a lateral position: i.e. hip externally rotated. This will also involve far less reaching and stretching for you because the medial aspect of the knee will be more exposed and better aligned to your corresponding hand.

♦ Use your inside hand to work from the inside of the leg. Slide your hand under the knee until your fingers and thumb form a 'U' shape supporting the hamstrings. Ensure the tips of your fingers and thumbs are level on each side.

♦ Apply a firm stroking movement towards the buttock before sweeping back to the starting position.

♦ If the movement is impeded because the client's leg is still resting on the chair, lift your supporting thigh forwards so the client's leg flexes more and lifts slightly off the chair.

Figure 10.61

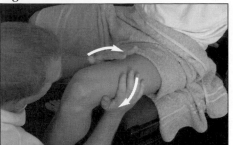

(a)

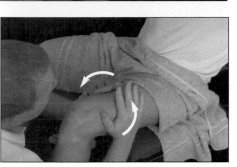

(b)

Shaking (Figure 10.61)

'Shaking' is used to induce a relaxed state in the muscles during pre-competition massages.

♦ *Starting position:* place the hands around the thigh with the heel of the hands gently gripping the hamstrings, which should be hanging loosely.

♦ Briskly rotate the hands from side to side to bring about a shaking action to the thigh.

♦ Post-competition massage ♦

After an athlete has finished an event their body needs time to recover. Post-competition massage aims to remove waste fluids from overused areas of the body to aid the recovery process. The most overused muscles of the body will suffer microtrauma from sustained exercise, and if the event was a contact sport, there will often be varying degrees of trauma to skin and muscles from physical impact.

Regardless of whether the event has involved contact, power, strength or endurance, the type of massage is the same. Often, there won't be any visible signs in the areas you suspect are traumatised. Massage these areas using plenty of effleurage and techniques that use only light pressure to ensure that you don't increase the trauma by damaging already weakened structures. Petrissage may be used with controlled and limited pressure over very bulky areas of muscles. Strokes should be slow and rhythmical to keep the circulation going while the athlete is cooling down, to help remove fluids and waste products and to prevent pooling in the muscles.

Chapter 11

Post-massage care

The responsibilities of the massage therapist may not end with practical applications on the massage couch. In conjunction with athletic trainers, coaches and medical professionals, the massage therapist will often become involved in implementing warm-up, cool-down and stretching programs.

The post-massage advice given by the sports massage therapist is therefore essential to the athlete in maintaining and improving their ability to perform sporting and everyday activities. Muscles in particular must be maintained in optimum condition. Thus, it is critical that the sports massage therapist has the knowledge to give the right advice and the ability to give clear instruction on how best to prepare the athlete for exercise and how to aid recovery. This means having a scientific understanding of, and practical skills relating to, the benefits of warming up, cooling down and stretching. The athlete may then enjoy the benefits of sports massage in helping restore normal function, as well as following up with the right programme to prepare the body for rigorous and competitive activity.

◆ The warm-up ◆

Light exercise undertaken in preparation for training or competition stimulates blood flow to the soft tissues, which increases the temperature and pliability of ligaments, tendons and muscles. This also helps to reduce muscle tension and may reduce the risk of injuring muscles while exercising. The warm-up also allows the athlete to prepare mentally for the session.

The warm-up session should last between 10 and 15 minutes. Where replication of the activity to follow is not possible, an activity such as jogging or the use of stationary rowing or cycling machines may be used. It should gradually increase in pace to prepare the body's systems for the intensity of the exercise in the main training session or competition.

◆ The cool-down ◆

All periods of intense physical exercise should finish with a cool-down that slowly decreases the intensity of the exercise before the athlete stops completely. A runner, for example, would cool down by jogging at a moderate pace for a few minutes, gradually slowing down to a walk before stopping and finishing the exercise session. As with the warm-up, the cool-down process should take 10–15 minutes.

Allowing the heart rate and circulation to slow down gradually prevents the pooling of blood and waste products in the muscles of the extremities. An abrupt halt after sustained exercise, may result in dizziness as blood pools in the legs. On rare occasions, elevated post-exercise levels of catecholamine (an adrenaline-like substance) may lead to dangerous heart arrhythmia, or abnormal rhythm, which may be avoided by a suitable cool-down. Stretching muscles during a cool-down is also important to improve flexibility, and may also reduce muscle soreness as discussed later in this chapter.

◆ Stretching – some ◆ general principles

Flexibility and range of motion

Flexibility is the range to which our muscular and connective tissues will allow a joint or group of joints to move in the 'absence of pain'. While there may be some mild discomfort at the extremes of a joint's action, pain is the body's way of saying that something has been, or is about to be, damaged. Stretching may therefore be considered to exist at the balance point between discomfort and damage.

Range of motion (ROM) – as discussed on p. 17 – is determined by the extensibility of muscular and connective tissues. Stretching soft tissue that is limiting the range of motion can improve flexibility and help reduce the risk of injury. *Hypermobility* and *laxity* are terms used in relation to flexibility to describe a joint with an abnormal ROM. Hypermobility describes the non-detrimental (either in terms of discomfort or performance), excess ROM beyond the accepted norm. Laxity describes the relative instability of a joint, regardless of its ROM, and the detrimental effect that this may have on comfort and/or performance.

Why is flexibility important for sports performance?

Healthy, supple muscle tissue that allows maximum 'normal' mobility contributes to optimum performance. This is because muscles in this condition are less prone to injury and facilitate greater ROM about the joints at which they act – therefore enabling enhanced performance. What 'normal' is in specific sports is determined by the demands of competition, and may often be considered abnormal in everyday life. For example, gymnasts may often be considered to be hypermobile, but their sport demands this for successful performance. Bear in mind, too, that tendons to which muscles attach have important recoil properties that generate considerable power, adding to ordinary muscle contraction. It may therefore be detrimental to have muscles that are too flexible.

If a muscle or joint is tight, it will progressively restrict motion as it approaches its maximum range. If an athlete's competitive actions requires that they approach this maximum range then their performance will not be optimal as they will be hampered at the extremes of their ROM. If they were more flexible they could perform with optimal speed and co-ordination throughout the desired ROM without approaching their maximal range. Second to this, it can be argued that most muscle injuries occur either during supramaximal loading or in supramaximal ranges of motion; extend the ROM, and the risk of exceeding it with any given action is reduced.

What happens to soft tissue when we stretch?

When soft tissue is stretched it changes shape. When the stretch is released, the soft tissue usually returns to its normal form. In these cases, and within the range that this occurs, the soft tissue is said to be *elastic* since it is capable of re-forming. This is particularly true of elastin fibres within the sarcolemma of the muscle. If the tissue is stretched beyond the elastic range (i.e. the elastic limit), the soft tissue does not re-form and will be permanently deformed. When the soft tissue loses its elasticity it is said to be *plastic*, and in the plastic range, the more the tissue is stretched, the greater the chance that any deformation will result in permanent damage. However, the collagen fibres of the muscles and connective tissues are plastic by nature. As such, they respond most readily to a static stretch of long duration (minimum 20–30 seconds) and low load (the stretch should not cause any significant discomfort).

Muscle reflexes

The body has mechanisms, called *muscle reflexes*, which help to prevent tissue deformation resulting from stretching overload, as described above. These are *reciprocal inhibition*, the *myostatic stretch reflex* and the *inverse stretch reflex*.

Reciprocal inhibition
In order that the body can move in a co-ordinated manner, the agonist and antagonist muscles (*see* p. 26) must communicate with one another in harmony. When the excitatory motor neurons of the agonist muscle initiate a given muscle action, an inhibitory impulse in the motor neurons of the antagonist muscle is triggered – so-called reciprocal inhibition. For example, during elbow flexion, the biceps contract and almost instantaneously the triceps relax. Thus, the active triceps stretch in Figure 11.4 (*see* p. 134), resulting from contraction of the biceps, is enhanced by the neurological inhibition of the triceps motor neurons.

The myostatic stretch reflex
Stretching a muscle lengthens both the muscle fibres and special receptors within the muscle called *muscle spindle fibres*. The muscle spindle fibres serve a protective function and respond to two sets of stimuli:

♦ how quickly the fibre is being stretched;
♦ how far the fibre is being stretched.

If a muscle is contracting too fast or too hard, it is the muscle spindle fibres of the *antagonist* muscle that are activated. For example, if the hamstrings are contracting rapidly towards full knee flexion then the muscle spindle fibres of the quadriceps will respond by contracting to prevent potential damage. It is therefore helpful to think of the myostatic stretch response as saving the active joint from damage as a result of rapid, forceful deformation at the end of its ROM.

A classic example of this is the knee jerk reflex: when the patellar tendon is tapped, the muscle spindle fibres of the quadriceps, located parallel to the muscle fibres, are stretched, causing them to deform. This causes the muscle spindles to fire, sending a message to the spinal cord. The brain returns an impulse to the quadriceps, causing them to contract to prevent any further stretching of the fibres. However, in a sporting environment it is usually the agonist–antagonist pairs that set up the tension rather than an external force.

The stretch reflex is likely to be activated during certain types of stretching, such as ballistic stretching, discussed later in this chapter.

Inverse stretch reflex

The inverse stretch reflex – also called *autogenic inhibition* – is similar to the myostatic stretch reflex. It involves sensory receptors called *Golgi tendon organs* (GTOs), which monitor degrees of tension within the skeletal muscle unit.

Rather than being located within the tendon itself, the vast majority of GTOs are actually situated within the musculo-tendinous junction of the muscle unit – its weakest point because this is where two tissue types merge, and therefore a common site of injury.

GTOs register contractile tension in the agonist muscle. As the muscle fibres contract, an increasing amount of tension is built up in the tendon as it delivers force to the bone. The GTOs initiate inhibitory impulses and these cause the agonist muscle to relax, releasing the tension in the musculo-tendinous junction and hence avoiding injury of the associated muscles, tendons, ligaments and joints. The inverse stretch reflex is thought to contribute to the effectiveness of proprioceptive neuro-muscular facilitation (PNF) stretching, as discussed later in this chapter.

What are the benefits of stretching to the athlete?

Mental relaxation

Stretching during the warm-up and cool-down allows the athlete to mentally relax and prepare or recover from the demands of physical activity.

Muscular relaxation

When the muscles are relaxed through stretching, tension is released and neuro-muscular functioning is improved, thus reducing the chances of injury.

Increased flexibility

Increasing flexibility and joint range of motion through a stretching programme can contribute to better sports performance.

Improved posture and balance in the musculo-skeletal system

Good posture is an important factor for healthy everyday living and optimum performance in sport. By adhering to a good stretching programme you may achieve better symmetry and a healthy balance throughout the musculo-skeletal system, which improves posture.

Prevention of lower back pain

After extensive study, Cailliet (1988) asserts that a 'mobilised, flexible and strengthened lumbar spine may help prevent lower back pain'.

Improved fitness

Supple muscles, healthy joint functioning, good range of motion and overall mobility all contribute to improved fitness, and all are improved by stretching.

Relief of muscle soreness

While the exact cause of *delayed onset of muscle soreness* (DOMS) is under investigation, Tillman and Cummings (1992) suggest that slow stretching exercises may reduce its effects. Following Howell et al. (1985), stretching may be most effective where DOMS is secondary to inflammatory or oedaemic response, rather

Cailliet, R. (1988), *Low Back Pain Syndrome* (4th ed.), (Philidelphia: F.A. Davis).

Tillman, L. J. and Cummings, G. S. (1992), 'Biological mechanisms of connective tissue mutability', in D. P. Carrier and R. M. Nelson (eds), *Dynamics of Human Biologic Tissues* (Philidephia: F. A. Davis), pp. 1–44.

Howell, J. N. et al (1985), 'An electromyographic study of elbow motion during post-exercise muscle soreness', *Journal of Applied Physiology*, **58**(5), pp. 1713–18.

than microtrauma to the protein myofilaments described in the sliding filament theory.

Relief of cramp

Involuntary muscle contraction of an already shortened muscle, commonly known as cramp, may be relieved by passively stretching the cramped muscle. (For a description of passive stretching, *see* pp. 129–30.)

Improved motor skills

Stretching improves motor skills by increasing flexibility, which is essential for skilled movement and conditioning – particularly in contact sports, dance and gymnastics.

Injury prevention

There is little conclusive research to support the contention that stretching reduces the occurrence of injury. However, the volume of observational data generated over the years by athletes, coaches and therapists has made the contention widely accepted, so much so that it is now demed to be unethical to ask a control group to participate in an activity study and not allow them to stretch. Returning to the concepts introduced on p. 125 *Why is flexibility important for sports performance?*, it becomes evident that injury prevention is an intuitively sound concept and that the muscles, tendons, ligaments and other joint structures can all be protected to some degree by a comprehensive stretching program.

Factors limiting flexibility

There are a variety of factors that may limit flexibility.

♦ The bony, ligamentous and capsular elements of the joint may define ROM.
♦ Skin, and especially scar issue, may limit the comfortable ROM of an activity. It is not uncommon to see 'stretch marks' on the skin

of the axillary regions of the pectorals of weightlifters. As much as they wish it were simply the muscles growing faster than the skin, it is more commonly over-stretching of the skin through 'flye'-type exercises that are to blame for the blemishes.

♦ In an increasingly sedentary population, where obesity is becoming prevalent, health professionals are finding it more and more difficult to take standard 'sit-and-reach' flexibility measures as pot-bellies get in the way of trunk flexion.
♦ Most relevant to the sports massage therapist are the limits of the muscle, fascia and tendons – the soft tissues with which they largely deal. These are discussed below.

Review of the structures of the sliding filament theory (*see* also p. 23) will show the sarcomere to be the basic unit of muscular contraction. The protein myofilaments of the sarcomere can only be stretched so far before they can no longer engage functionally or are damaged. The elastin fibres of the sarcolemma are highly resilient, but they too may be torn if stretched too far. At the higher levels of organisation in the skeletal muscle unit, the plastic nature of the collagen fibres of the tendon, fascia/epimysium, perimysium and endomysium limit flexibility. One area of muscular limitation that is often overlooked is that of simple mechanical block – the muscle mass is such that it prevents other limitations from being reached. Think of a sprinters calves and hamstrings meeting on a forced knee flexion, stopping that motion well before the joint capsule is stressed.

The processes of muscle atrophy through decreased activity, immobilisation due to injury or ageing can all negatively affect flexibility. The atrophy of the muscle tissue is accompanied by inclusion of collagen fibres in areas previously dominated by elastin fibres. Consequently, the plastic nature of collagen replaces the elastic properties of elastin and the flexibility of the skeletal muscle unit decreases to reflect this change.

♦ Types of stretching ♦

The following section introduces seven major types of stretching. Of these, only the assisted and PNF stretches require the physical assistance of the massage therapist. The remaining types require that the therapist instruct and observe to ensure that the athlete performs the stretches safely and accurately. Once proper stretching techniques are ingrained in the athlete, the massage therapist may occasionally reassess the athlete to determine that good form has been maintained – adjusting the exercises of the stretching programme to meet their current needs.

Static stretching

Static stretching involves taking a joint through its range to a point where the soft tissue is comfortably stretched and then holding the position for a period of time. Short-duration (6–10 seconds) static stretching is referred to as 'maintenance stretching' and is used most commonly during a workout to return the muscle to its pre-activity length. Long duration (20–30 seconds) static stretching is referred to as 'developmental stretching' and is most commonly incorporated into the cool-down to increase muscle length beyond its usual range of motion – thus actively increasing flexibility. For example, during a workout an athlete may do a standing hamstring maintenance stretch between sprints; while at the end of the session, they may do a lying hamstring developmental stretch as it would be easier to hold the stretch while comfortably on the ground.

There is an increasing benefit in holding the developmental stretch for longer duration, but there is also a point of diminishing returns where the time spent simply does not justify the almost immeasurable extra gains in flexibility. Similarly, repeated stretches to the same muscle will give diminishing returns. A good balance between time and results is three stretches of 30 seconds per muscle. A rest of 10–15 seconds between stretches is sufficient. Static stretching works largely by mechanical means affecting the elastin and collagen fibres of the skeletal muscle unit.

Active stretching

In active stretching the client activates an isometric contraction (where force is exerted but muscle length does not change) at the full inner position of the joint – promoting the stretch, at extension, of the antagonist muscle or group. For example, fully contracting the hamstrings to full knee flexion will encourage a mechanical stretch of the quadriceps which will be enhanced by reciprocal inhibition (*see* p. 126). This type of stretching is useful for dancers and martial artists or others who need strength at extreme ranges of motion.

Passive stretching

Passive stretching is distinguished from assisted stretching (*see* below) by the absence (passive) or presence (assisted) of the sports massage therapist. It will be further differentiated from static stretching by the addition of extra force. In passive stretching the client uses a prop to exert a force in order to extend or deepen a stretch. The prop may be as simple as using hand and arm strength to deepen a hamstring stretch, or a towel hooked over the heel to draw the leg into a deeper stretch. This is an effective way to deepen a static stretch, as the client is in control at all times.

Assisted stretching

Assisted stretching is where the client is instructed to relax the muscles and the therapist moves the joint through its range to its comfortable limit. This is particularly useful when used in conjunction with sports massage to assess periodically the effects of massage, as well as to improve flexibility. It is most important to give clear instructions and request feedback from your client to ensure that no harm is done during the stretch.

Dynamic stretching

Dynamic stretching is a controlled, rhythmic, repeated motion to the point of tension and return to full inner position. For example, from a seated position, extend one leg in front of you and draw the toes towards the knee (dorsiflexion) until tension is felt; return to full toe point (plantarflexion) and repeat 10 times. Each motion should take at least three seconds. By using controlled movements, this type of stretching also lubricates the joints by stimulating the production of synovial fluid. The combination of light activity, musculo-tendinous stretching and joint lubrication produces a combination of warm-up and stretching that is known as *mobilisation*.

Ballistic stretching

Ballistic stretching refers to a rapid, acceler-ative, repeated action beyond normal ROM with a slow return to the start position. It is the most controversial form of stretching, as it can inappropriately trigger muscle reflexes and/or cause damage to the skeletal muscle unit or associated joint structures. It is necessary only in sport-specific instances where the decelerative muscle is at risk of injury in explosive activities – for example,

the hamstrings are at risk of injury when they decelerate the knee as it approaches full extension during hurdling activities. Sprinters, hurdlers, martial artists and throwers are athletes who may need to incorporate ballistic stretching into their routines. This would follow other warm-up and stretching activities to prepare the tissue.

Proprioceptive neuromuscular facilitation (PNF)

There are several methods of PNF, based on the theory that a muscle will be most effectively stretched if neurological stimuli are fully integrated into the mechanical aspects of stretching. At least nine forms of PNF are described in the literature, with hold–relax (HR), contract–relax (CR) and contract–relax–antagonist–contract (CRAC) being the most widely practised.

It is strongly recommended that a therapist undertake supervised instruction in the 'art and science' of PNF, as it is very easily misunderstood and ineffectively applied when taken directly from a book. That being said, a brief introduction to the three common forms of PNF follows.

Hold–relax (HR) PNF
This is based on a combination of active and assisted stretching (*see* above). For example, to stretch the hamstrings, the client actively stretches (holds) the hamstrings via the contraction of the quadriceps and hip flexors for 6–10 seconds. The client then relaxes as the therapist assists the limb to its new maximum ROM over the course of 6–10 seconds. Three repetitions of the cycle will suffice.

This type of PNF is most effective when the client has limited and/or painful ROM. The client will often be sedentary, elderly or in injury rehabilitation. Advantages include the strengthening of the antagonist muscle during the active/hold portion of the stretch; increased flexibility and muscular co-ordination is also encouraged through the activation of reciprocal inhibition via reciprocal innervation (see p. 126). Risks are related to the assisted portion of the stretch.

Contract–relax (CR) PNF

This is based on a combination of isometric resistance and assisted stretching (*see* above). For an example we will again look at the hamstrings. From the point of tension, the client applies pressure against the therapist who resists the hamstrings' attempts to flex the knee and extend the hip. Over the course of about four seconds the client builds from 30 per cent to 70 per cent contraction and then holds for a further six seconds. As the client relaxes, the therapist assists the limb to its new maximum ROM over the course of 6–10 seconds. Three repetitions will suffice.

This type of stretching is most effective when the client has limited, pain-free ROM. The client will often be sedentary, elderly or at a late stage in injury rehabilitation. Advantages include the strengthening of the stretched muscle during the contract portion of the stretch, and increased flexibility encouraged through the activation of the inverse stretch reflex via the Golgi tendon organs (*see* p. 127). Risks are related to the assisted portion of the stretch.

Contract–relax–antagonist–contract (CRAC) PNF

This is based on a combination of isometric resistance and active stretching (*see* above). For consistency in the examples we will again look at the hamstrings. From the point of tension, the client applies pressure against the therapist who resists the hamstrings', attempts to flex the knee and extend the hip. Over the course of about four seconds the client builds from 30 per cent to 70 per cent contraction and then holds for a further six seconds. As the client relaxes, they will change to an active stretch at the limb's new maximum ROM and hold for 6–10 seconds. The therapist follows the limb to its new position in preparation for the next resistance of isometric contraction. Three repetitions of the cycle will suffice.

This type of stretching is possibly the most effective form of developmental stretching. Advantages include the strengthening of the stretched muscle during the contract portion of the stretch, and increased flexibility encouraged through the activation of the inverse stretch reflex via the Golgi tendon organs – as well as the activation of reciprocal inhibition via reciprocal innervation (*see* p. 126). Risks are minimised as the client is in control of the strength of contraction in both the isometric resistance and active stretch portions of the PNF stretch cycle.

Table 11.1 Summary of stretching terms

Term	Definition
Flexibility	Normal, physiological ROM of joint or limb
Hypermobility	Non-detrimental excess ROM of joint or limb
Laxity	Relative instability of joint or limb regardless of ROM
Stretch	Lengthening the soft/connective tissue of a joint
♦ Static	Controlled hold at end of normal ROM
♦ Static maintenance	Hold 10–15 seconds to maintain flexibility
♦ Static developmental	Hold 20–30 seconds to increase flexibility
♦ Active	Isometric contraction of the antagonist muscle
♦ Passive	Use of self or prop to deepen a stretch
♦ Assisted	Use of partner to deepen a stretch
♦ Dynamic	Controlled, repeated motion to end of normal ROM
♦ Ballistic	Quick, repeated motion beyond end of normal ROM
♦ PNF	Proprioceptive neuromuscular facilitation

♦ The stretches ♦

The static stretches illustrated in this section cover all the major muscle groups in the body and may be useful for your client. Instructions and teaching points are provided for each exercise.

Upper body

Pectorals and anterior deltoids (chest) – Figure 11.1
Starting position and instructions
Stand with your arms stretched out to the side as illustrated. Keep the elbows slightly flexed and the hands level with the shoulders. With thumbs pointing downwards, gently draw your shoulder blades together at the back.

Teaching points
♦ Be careful to maintain the natural lumbar curve.
♦ Keep the thumbs down, or you may place undue tension on the biceps – thus limiting the stretch in the chest.

Figure 11.1

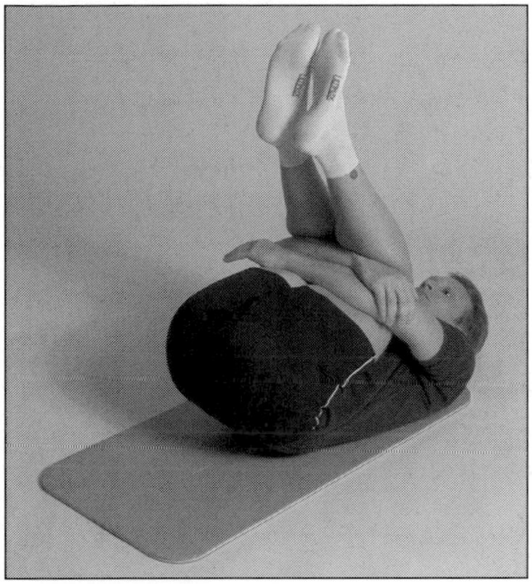

Figure 11.2

Figure 11.3

Alternative position

Stand facing into the corner of a room, or a doorway. Raise your arms to shoulder height and, with elbows bent, place your forearms flat on the wall or door frame. Gently, lower your body weight into the corner or through the doorway.

Erector spinae and multifidus (lower back) – Figure 11.2
Starting position and instructions

Lie supine (on your back) on the floor. Flex your knees and draw your feet towards the buttocks, maintaining contact with the floor. Using your abdominal muscles, draw the feet off the floor, knees towards chest. Think of lifting your lower back, vertebra by vertebra, from the floor. Reach forwards with both hands and grasp your knees. Gently continue to draw the knees into the chest, using your hands to help you.

Teaching points

♦ Make sure that this is a gentle stretch – there is no need to rock.

Alternative position – the 'cat stretch'

On your hands and knees, arch (flex) your spine towards the ceiling – just like a cat. Return gently to the 'flat' position. Do not let the back drop below this flat position (hyperextend).

Latissimus dorsi (back) – Figure 11.3
Starting position and instructions

Extend your arms overhead, grasping one wrist with the opposite hand. Gently draw the grasped arm higher into the air. Lean slightly away from it, and then draw the arm across an imaginary centre line above the head.

Teaching points

♦ Avoid locking the fingers together.
♦ Avoid locking the elbows.
♦ Maintain the natural lumbar curve.
♦ Hold your head in a 'neutral' position; do not allow it to drop forwards.

Alternative position

Lie supine (on your back) on the floor with your arms by your sides. Slowly raise and extend one arm above your head and back towards the floor. Lead with the little finger. Do not allow your lower back to arch.

Figure 11.4

Triceps (back of arms) – Figure 11.4
Starting position and instructions
Raise and extend your right arm with your palm facing backwards. Flex your elbow so that your hand rests between your shoulder blades and, placing your left hand as illustrated, exert a gentle backwards pressure until you feel a mild stretch in the right triceps. Repeat on the left.

Teaching points
♦ Maintain the natural lumbar curve.
♦ Keep the head in a 'neutral' position; do not allow it to drop too far forwards.
♦ The arms should 'slice' back close to the ears.

Alternative position
Raise and extend both arms. As they reach the vertical, place the palms together. Flex your elbows and reach behind your head towards the shoulder blades. As your hands pass behind your head, turn them so that the palms face away from one another. Reach deeper between the shoulder blades.

Rhomboids (upper back) – Figure 11.5
Starting position and instructions
Reach your arms in front of your body and overlap hands. Flex the elbows out to the side and try to hug an imaginary, 'expanding' tree or large barrel. As you reach around the imaginary object, try to draw the shoulder blades apart.

Teaching points
♦ Maintain the natural lumbar curve.
♦ Keep your head in the 'neutral' position, lifting the chin off the chest.
♦ Avoid interlocking your fingers.

Alternative position
Stand tall with your arms at your side, and try to round the shoulders forwards.

Figure 11.5

Figure 11.6

Medial and posterior deltoids (back of shoulder) – Figure 11.6

Stand tall and draw one arm across your body at chest to shoulder level. Grasp that arm above the elbow with your opposite hand, and gently pull it closer to your body. Repeat on the other side.

Teaching points

♦ Avoid rotating the trunk.
♦ The assisting hand should be above the elbow of the arm being stretched.

Alternative position

Try elevating or dropping the 'target' arm slightly, to find the optimal point of tension.

Figure 11.7

Anterior deltoids (front of shoulder) – Figure 11.7

Starting position and instructions

Stand tall and extend your arms behind your body. Overlap the hands and gently draw them higher behind the body.

Teaching points

♦ Avoid leaning forwards at the waist.
♦ Keep the head in a 'neutral' position; lift your chin off your chest.
♦ Don't interlock your fingers.
♦ Your elbows may bend slightly.

Alternative position

If this area is particularly tight, grasp a towel between your hands and raise both arms together – with space between the hands.

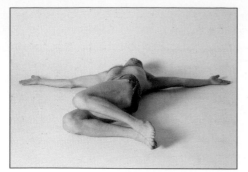

Figure 11.8

Obliques (side of waist) – Figure 11.8
Starting position and instructions
Lie supine (on your back) on the floor. Draw the heels of your feet towards the buttocks, while maintaining contact with both the soles of your feet, and with your lower back. Stretch your arms out to the side at shoulder level. Slowly lower your knees to one side and hold. Return to the centre position and repeat on the opposite side.

Teaching points
♦ Keep your ankles and knees together as you lower to the side.
♦ Pause in the upright position before going to the opposite side.

Alternative position
Once in the side-rotated position, extend the upper leg and point the toes to increase the stretch.

Lower body

Figure 11.9

Quadriceps (front of thighs) – Figure 11.9
Starting position and instructions
Standing tall on one leg, and using a wall for balance if necessary, flex the other knee and grip the shin or ankle – rather than the foot, to avoid plantarflexion – with the hand on the same side. Push your hip forwards to achieve a stretch (rather than pulling your foot towards your buttock).

Teaching points
♦ Avoid leaning forwards at the waist.
♦ Keep your thighs close together and the knee of the target leg pointing towards the floor.
♦ Think about hip forwards rather than 'heel to bottom'.

Alternative position
Try the stretch lying on your side, with the target leg uppermost.

Figure 11.10

Hamstrings (back of thighs) – Figure 11.10
Starting position and instructions
Stand with your feet staggered front to back, as shown. Keep the knee of the front leg straight. Flex the knee of your rear leg and lower the buttocks towards the floor. Place your hands on the thigh of the bent leg for support. Rather than bending forwards to deepen the stretch, raise your buttocks back and up.
Teaching points
♦ Push your bottom back and up to increase the stretch.
♦ Avoid bending at the waist.
♦ Keep the foot of the target leg flat on the floor.
Alternative position
Lie supine (on your back) and elevate the target leg using your hands to gently increase stretch.

Figure 11.11

Gluteals (buttocks) and Ilio tibial band – Figure 11.11
Starting position and instructions
Sit with your legs stretched out in front of you. Flex the knee of one leg, drawing the foot towards the buttock, with the sole of the foot flat on the floor. When the foot of the bent leg approaches the knee of the straight leg, lift the foot of the bent leg over the straight leg and place it flat on the floor – with that ankle touching the outside of the straight leg. Sit tall and, with hands embracing the bent knee, draw the bent leg towards the chest.
Teaching points
♦ Sit tall and avoid rotation of the spine.
♦ Draw the knee to the chest gently.
Alternative position – 'Figure Four'
Lie supine (on your back) and bend your knees to 90 degrees, with the soles of your feet flat on the floor. Raise one leg and rest the outside of that ankle on the front of the knee that remains bent at 90 degrees. Place the hand on the side of the raised leg through the hole created between the legs. With the hand on the side of the bent leg, reach past the outside of the bent leg and grasp the opposite hand around the back of the bent leg. Gently draw the legs towards the chest.

Figure 11.12

Iliopsoas and rectus femoris (hip flexors) – *Figure 11.12*
Starting position and instructions

Assume a deep lunge position, with the lead foot extended so that knee flexion exceeds 90 degrees. The trail leg should contact the floor at the knee and the foot. The toes of the trail foot point towards the midline of the body. Keep your body tall and the lumbar curve natural. Rock forwards onto the lead leg, gently driving forwards from the hips. Keep the knee of the lead leg over the lead foot.

Teaching points
♦ Keep the knee of your target (trail) leg on the ground, with the toes pointing in.
♦ Keep your hips square and forward-facing.
♦ Avoid bending forwards at the waist.

Alternative position

Sit sideways on a chair with a high back. One buttock remains on the seat of chair, while the other is off the edge. Lean forwards at the waist and extend the hanging leg behind your body, keeping the top of the foot in contact with the floor, and your toes pointing towards the midline. Raise your body up to a vertical position, avoiding hyperextension of the lower back.

Figure 11.13(a)

Adductors (inner thighs) – *Figure 11.13*
Starting position and instructions

Sit tall with your legs outstretched. Draw your heels towards your buttocks, while letting the knees fall outwards and the soles of the feet come together. Press your knees gently towards the floor. Your hands can rest comfortably in any postion that feels natural; or be used to push down gently on the knees to assist the stretch.

Teaching points
♦ Sit tall and avoid slouching forwards.
♦ Let gravity do the work; there is no need to force the knees to the floor, unless you are extremely supple.

Figure 11.13(b)

Alternative position
Assume the same position, but straighten your legs to produce a wide 'V' in front of your body. This will include the gracilis muscle.

Figure 11.14

Gastrocnemius (upper calves) – Figure 11.14
Starting position and instructions
Stand tall with your feet widely staggered front to back. Keep the trail leg straight. Flex the knee of the lead leg and lean forwards over it. Your hands may rest on the lead leg or any stable structure (for example, a wall, chair or railing). Keep your feet in line with one another and pointing forwards.

Teaching points
♦ Keep the trail leg straight throughout the stretch.
♦ The heel of the trail leg stays in contact with the floor.

Alternative position
Stand on a step or ledge with your heels hanging free. With your knees straight, lower one heel at a time off the step or ledge.

Soleus (lower calves) – Figure 11.15
Starting position and instructions
As for Figure 11.14 above, but with the trail leg flexed slightly at the knee.

Figure 11.15

Chapter 12

Injury management

Unfortunately, even when all the correct preparations are made and maximum safety precautions taken, injuries still occur in sport – due perhaps to extreme weather conditions, limited physical endurance, or physical contact. It is therefore important that qualified first aid officers are available at sports venues. Prompt and correct first aid management will often have a vital bearing on keeping the rehabilitation period to a minimum and ensuring a full and successful recovery for the athlete. As a sports massage therapist you may often be asked to attend sporting competitions to help individual clients – or whole teams of players – by providing sports massage. You must, therefore, be skilled in the application of first aid treatments when attending events where there is an increased risk of players being injured. Knowledge in this area will also enable you to advise your clients on what to do for themselves if they are injured and you are not there to help.

This chapter discusses the physiological changes which occur in the body as a direct result of injury, and how the sports massage therapist can manage the injury to encourage the best recovery possible. In the next chapter we look at sporting events and how we can manage and respond to the environment to help prevent injury and enhance safety in sport.

◆ What is injury ◆ management?

Although this book is about sports massage, it is important to understand what happens when tissue is damaged so you can decide on what is the appropriate treatment or action for your client. Injury management is not only about providing sound treatment – it is as much about 'managing' the athlete so that their actions help to reduce inflammation and the risk of further injury, and promote recovery.

To provide the best care for your client, this often means using other modalities such as stretching, correctional exercises, strength work and electrotherapy, in addition to sports massage. You should not attempt to diagnose and treat all conditions. Sports massage therapists must work within the limitations of their training like any other professional involved in sports medicine. However, once you can recognise the signs and symptoms of injury, you will be able to give first aid treatment – and often make sound recommendations on the athlete's next course of action.

In cases where an injury requires you to refer your client on to a specialist, there will often be a period of time between the initial detection of the condition and the specialist's next available appointment. It will benefit your client if you can manage the injury during this period and possibly help the recovery process. There may also be occasions when your client will benefit from sports massage at the same time as receiving treatment elsewhere.

There are well-documented methods of managing an injury, depending on how long it is since the injury occurred. You must be familiar with the guidelines on healing times, which are divided into phases, and how the effects of sports massage will benefit your client during these phases. Both will be discussed in detail in this chapter.

♦ Types of injuries ♦

There are two main classifications of injuries:

♦ *Intrinsic* injuries are those caused by a sudden or consistent change in internal forces, causing a sudden or 'incidental' injury such as a muscle 'pull' or tear. They may also be caused by repeated excessive force resulting in overuse, causing inflammation, stress fractures or tissue degeneration.
♦ *Extrinsic* or traumatic injuries result from the collision of the body with an external force such as an object or the ground. Typical extrinsic injuries are contusions, fractures and dislocations. Athletes may also suffer extrinsic overuse conditions such as blisters.

In many instances when soft tissue is damaged, no matter how small the injury, it will have either been stretched or, if an impact was involved, various structures will have been torn. Even if the injury is minor, it is likely that the blood vessels feeding nutrients to the tissue and other structures will also be damaged. The amount of bleeding will depend on the vascularity of the tissue involved, and will be increased if the injury happened during exercise.

♦ Stages of the healing ♦ process

It is not possible to give exact time constraints for healing, because there are several factors that influence the speed of repair. However, there is a definite sequence of events. Much depends on the severity of the injury, the age of the injured athlete, how fit the athlete was at the time of injury, and what they do to encourage their body to recover. For example, as people age, their metabolic rates slow down and resolution takes longer (*see* also pp. 43–4). As mentioned above, there are guidelines on healing times for injuries, which are divided into the follow phases:

♦ The *acute* or *inflammatory phase* – from the time of injury up to four or five days afterwards.
♦ The *repair phase* – from 48 hours up to several weeks after injury.
♦ The *remodelling phase* – from three weeks up to a year after injury.

These phases and the processes which occur under each do overlap and are continuous processes. So, the acute inflammatory phase will often continue after the repair processes have begun.

The acute phase

The first stage immediately following injury is known as the acute, or inflammatory phase. This lasts for several days after injury and is often characterised by the following signs and symptoms (usually begin within 24 hours):

♦ Pain
♦ Heat
♦ Redness
♦ Swelling
♦ Loss of normal function

Swelling may be caused by damaged blood vessels leaking blood into the tissues, sometimes causing discoloration on the surface. The first reflex action (lasting anything from a few seconds to 10 minutes) resulting from damage and pain at the site of an injury involves vaso-constriction, which helps to reduce blood loss from the damaged vessels. However, this also leads to cells being starved of nourishment because of poor blood supply and they soon die. These dying cells release a substance called *histamine*, which causes the blood vessels to dilate – bringing increased blood supply and extra nutrients to help repair and rebuild the damaged tissue. The dead cells and blood from broken vessels form a haematoma (or bruise) and must be cleared from the tissue to allow the healing process to commence properly.

During this phase the blood capillary walls become dilated and more permeable. The increased blood supply becomes more viscous and therefore slower. As the pressure increases, plasma is forced through the capillary walls into the interstitial spaces. Specialised white blood cells migrate to the area to ingest dead cells and debris, and fight infection. If the area becomes infected this often causes redness and heat and if the infection continues, more white blood cells move to the affected site until the infection has been overcome. As the inflammatory phase progresses, a very fine 'fibrin' mesh* is laid down as the first building structure of the repair process.

Muscle spasm may also occur during the acute phase as part of the body's protective mechanism (*see* also p. 56). This causes the

muscle to contract involuntarily, increasing the tension in the muscle and limiting further movement. However, this may have an adverse effect on the injury by restricting blood flow, placing more pressure on nerve endings and causing more pain. Injury management aims at breaking the cycle of pain, pressure on nerves, and spasm.

The action taken (or not taken) during the early stages following an injury will have a direct effect on how long it takes the athlete to recover and ultimately return to competitive sport. The speed with which bleeding can be slowed down and debris cleared from the site of injury will influence how quickly recovery will start. Damaged blood vessels are plugged and healed within the first 48 to 72 hours, so the immediate action taken is to restrict blood loss from the vessels – described below.

Treatment during the acute phase

The therapist's aim immediately after injury is to aid narrowing of the blood vessels (vaso-constriction), stem the flow of blood, and reduce the amount of inflammation. By applying ice or cooling immediately after an injury, the level of swelling and amount of blood allowed to leak out may be reduced. Compression and elevation (*see* below) will also assist this. This treatment is remembered by the commonly used acronym 'RICE', which stands for Rest, Ice, Compression and Elevation.

It is important to be able to give first aid treatment as soon as possible following injury. This is usually on the field of play – although this depends on the sport, since the first priority may be to remove the injured competitior from further danger (for example, from the path of an oncoming cyclist). For more information, *see* Chapter 13 on attending sports events.

*Very fine, hair-like structures which are very weak, but also bridge gaps in damaged tissue to allow adherence of other structures in the repair process. It is therefore very important for the athlete to rest during this period, to allow this mesh to become strong enough to withstand stress.

Rest

Rest the injured part immediately to prevent further damage. This means ceasing the activity immediately and moving the injured area as little as possible. After the acute phase, encourage your client to exercise the rest of the body to maintain some fitness while injured.

Ice

Apply ice as soon as possible, for 10–12 minutes, to slow down the inflammation – do not wait for the swelling to start. This causes a reflex action which narrows the blood vessels supplying the area and therefore reduces blood flow. Because it is a reflex action the ice may only cool the superficial tissue to gain the desired effect in the underlying muscle.

Reapply ice every one to two hours during the acute phase. It is important not to keep the ice on any longer than the time stated above, because after this time, the body would react by dilating the blood vessels and increasing blood flow to warm the cold tissue and stop the cells dying. This would lead to more blood leaking into the interstitial spaces, which in turn would exacerbate the swelling. Never apply ice directly on to the skin, as this may result in ice burns. Wrap the ice in a damp cloth (a dry cloth will not transmit cold effectively). The cooling also produces an analgesic effect which helps to reduce muscle spasm. (Once the effects have taken place the athlete must not be tempted to continue playing because the pain has been relieved.)

Compression

Apply a compression bandage (usually a crepe bandage) to help minimise the swelling of the tissue. Ensure that this is applied firmly, but is not too tight. Attach the bandage in a distal to proximal direction, making sure that it covers an area both proximal and distal to the site of the injury to contain the swelling. This will also keep any swelling away from any distal extremities. Compression helps prevent oedema (an abnormally high amount of fluid in the tissue) by increasing the pressure on the tissues and therefore limiting the amount of fluid which can enter the area.

Elevation

Elevate the injured area to reduce blood flow and limit the use of associated muscles. The capillary hydrostatic pressure is also reduced, which decreases the amount of fluid forced into the interstitial spaces.

There is much debate and conflicting research about which of the above actions is most effective. None need be forfeited for any of the others, and it is therefore sensible to recommend that all procedures are followed for the first 48 to 72 hours following injury. This will depend on the severity of the injury, and applies to players who may not be directly under your care during the first 48–72 hours. Others who are may be reassessed every few hours during the acute stage.

Failure to follow the RICE procedure will mean that the recovery period from injury may be considerably extended while the swelling and removal of dead tissue and

---

When is the use of ice contraindicated?

♦ Never apply ice directly to the skin. This may cause frostbite and burn the skin.

♦ Do not use ice if it causes pain. Some people are very sensitive to the application of ice.

♦ Do not use ice on injuries in the chest region. This may limit arterial blood flow to the heart.

♦ If a person cannot feel touch before applying ice, this may indicate other problems such as nerve impingement. In such instances ice would only serve to mask this and complicate the problem.

blood cells are dealt with by the body. If the injury is not properly managed and these waste products are not removed, long-term problems may be created for the athlete as the debris and fluid begin to congeal and solidify.

No massage must be carried out during the first 48-72 hours of the acute phase, and no heat applied. Recently repaired healed blood vessels will be re-opened and massage will cause vaso-dilation and restart the bleeding.

The repair phase

The inflammatory phase subsides any time after the first two days and, as swelling reduces, the repair process begins. By now the blood vessels will have repaired and the transportation of nutrients and oxygen to the tissue will have been restored. Muscle does not have the ability to produce new tissue, but replaces damaged areas with scar tissue. This commences with the formation of a highly vascular mass of cells capable of producing the repair tissue known as *collagen*. Over the next two to four weeks this very weak connective tissue gains more collagen fibres and becomes stronger, while losing its vascularity.

As scar tissue develops it becomes fibrous and inelastic. This new tissue is neither as functional nor as strong as healthy muscle: scar tissue is estimated to reach only 70 per cent of the tensile strength of surrounding muscle tissue and so a weak and vulnerable area develops at the site of repair. It also shrinks by up to 30 per cent as its formation continues and it is therefore important that the athlete starts exercising and stretching in the repair phase in order to make the whole muscle including the newly formed tissue, both strong and supple.

Treatment during the repair phase

The sports massage therapist should explain to the injured athlete how important it is for them to follow the advice given below to promote an early recovery and return to sport. Even though the blood vessels will have repaired by now, damaged muscle fibres and connective tissue will still be weak. Although different exercises may be used to increase mobility – and later strength – in the early stages they must be used cautiously, ensuring that there is no discomfort. Any pain is a clear sign that the repairing tissues are being damaged again, extending the recovery period. Appropriate exercises for this stage in the healing process are described below. There may still be an inflammatory response during this phase; this can be contained by the continued use of a compression bandage.

During the repair phase, ice massage may be incorporated into treatments along with the exercises described below. By applying stroking movements with an ice pack, the blood vessels will dilate and constrict – increasing the supply of blood and nutrients to the area, increasing the rate of healing, and reducing the amount of pain and discomfort. Advise the injured athlete to apply an ice pack to the affected area for 15–20 minutes and to try gentle, pain-free movements. By cooling the area for a longer time than during the acute phase (*see* above), the body reacts by increasing the circulation to the injured area to warm up the tissue, preventing lasting damage to the cells.

Massage during this phase might include light effleurage (*see* Chapter 9, pp. 81–2) to encourage circulation, stimulate the healing process and reduce swelling.

Exercises appropriate to the repair phase
As a general rule, advise the athlete to start static stretches in the pain-free range on, or after, the fourth day following the injury. By

gently stretching the damaged muscle, new structures which are being formed during the repair process are aligned in the direction of the existing fibres. The result is a much healthier and stronger structure when the rehabilitation period is complete. Stretching is also known to increase circulation, improve suppleness in the muscle tissue, increase overall flexibility, and improve the range of motion of the affected joints. Early joint mobilisation will also encourage production of synovial fluid, which will nourish and lubricate the joint. For more information on static stretching, *see* Chapter 11, p. 129.

As well as encouraging a healthier alignment of repair tissue through stretching, strength must be restored to the injured area. Muscle contraction and increased loading may progress within the pain-free range and must be encouraged for some time if scar tissue formation is suspected. In these instances it is difficult for the muscle to regain its former strength because of the non-contractile scar tissue. An extensive weight training and resistance programme is recommended, with the aim of regaining sufficient strength before considering re-entering competition. This should start with static muscle contractions some days after injury, and progress to resistance work with increasing joint movements and gradually increasing levels of resistance over the next four to five weeks. The strength work will begin with light resistance (non-weight-bearing) training, increasing – both in terms of resistance and joint range of motion – as strength returns. For more information on this subject, *see The Complete Guide to Strength Training* by Anita Bean (A & C Black).

Finally, think of alternative exercises for your client that will not put excessive stresses on the injured area. This may help your client resist the temptation to return to sport too soon. Exercise in water is often a suitable alternative, but should be accompanied by specific instructions – some swimming strokes as well as poor swimming technique may prove detrimental to certain conditions (for example, breaststroke is generally contraindicated for anyone suffering from back problems).

The remodelling phase

The final phase of healing is known as the remodelling phase, which takes place from about three weeks up to a year after the injury. During this time, cell activity returns to normal and the scar tissue matures along the lines of mechanical stress applied during the specific stretching and resistance exercises described above. As scar tissue develops you may use deeper and firmer massage techniques to stretch the newly formed collagen fibres in the direction of the muscle fibres.

Tendons and ligaments have poorer healing qualities than muscle tissue because they have a poorer blood supply and may therefore take much longer to heal – depending on the type and severity of the injury. Ligament damage may result in joint instability. Muscles, tendons and ligaments all respond to levels of mechanical stress and therefore immobilisation and inactivity lead to atrophy and loss of strength – so strengthening exercises should be introduced as soon as possible to stimulate the healing process and hypertrophy (*see* p. 39).

♦ When can the athlete return ♦ to competitive sport?

Many athletes return to competitive sport too soon, due either to overenthusiasm or pressure from a coach or manager. The result may be that poor reflex actions, lower skill levels or premature fatigue make them more vulnerable to further injury. This risk of suffering the same injury, or a secondary injury that is more severe, is greater in contact sports.

Prior to returning to competitive sport, the injured area and the athlete's overall fitness should be assessed in the following ways.

♦ The injured area must be thoroughly tested with specific exercises of increasing intensity that at least match the stresses they will undergo when competing.

♦ Tissue strength, flexibility and the range of motion of any affected joints must be restored, although not necessarily to the pre-injury level as this is not always possible.

The appropriate specialist – i.e. whoever *diagnosed* the injury – must decide what is acceptable under the circumstances. Flexibility, strength and mobility should be compared closely with the corresponding symmetrical part of the body.

♦ The athlete must regain their overall fitness, enabling them to undergo the rigours of full competition. This will involve testing their stamina, suppleness, skills, speed, and strength relative to the demands of their chosen sport. Only when the athlete achieves acceptable levels in all of these fitness components should they be allowed to compete again.

Chapter 13

Working at sports events

Working at sports events should present you with some of your most memorable experiences as a sports massage therapist, and with opportunities to make contact with potential clients. You will be required to work in busier surroundings, in a less structured way, and under some pressure, but being part of a team and working in a competitive atmosphere can provide you with a real boost to morale – and the experience is invaluable. This chapter focuses on how you should prepare for and conduct yourself at these events, to ensure that they are a success. You may also become involved in checking the safety conditions at sports events, so guidelines on checking safety factors are also detailed.

♦ How can I get involved ♦

Many sports magazines and local newspapers contain advertisements for competitions taking place all over the country, for both amateur and professional athletes. Find out who is in charge of the event and talk to them directly. Explain what services you can provide as a sports massage therapist and how the event participants can benefit. Event organisers are always eager to add ways to draw more people to their competitions, and sports massage is a great attraction. This is especially true for athletes who compete regularly, so the sports massage service may

be one way to encourage them to return to the same event year after year.

♦ Preparing for a sports event ♦

There are several tasks which you need to complete beforehand to ensure that the whole event goes smoothly for you and for your clients.

Do your homework

First, always do your homework before the event and find out as much as possible about the sport and activities involved, especially if they are unfamiliar to you. This will ensure that you have a thorough understanding of the physical and mental demands involved, and will provide you with a valuable insight into the potential target areas for your sports massage on the day. Improving your knowledge of the sport in question will also give you the added advantage of being able to communicate on equal terms with the competitors and personnel involved.

Clarify your responsibilities

Liaise with event organisers to ensure that your responsibilities are clearly defined. If what is required is beyond your level of training, emphasise that you are not qualified to undertake certain aspects – this is very important, so that everyone is aware of your level of expertise and you are not expected to carry out responsibilities for which you are not trained, such as first aid treatment or injury care.

Confirm arrangements and finances

Confirm all agreements and financial arrangements in advance. Many sports have limited funding so it is unlikely that you will be paid for your services. However, you can expect the organisers to provide food and refreshments on the day, and to contribute to reasonable travelling expenses. Confirm this with them and give them an estimate of your expenses. Avoiding any misunderstanding increases the probability of being invited back to future events. If you intend charging the participants a fee you will need to check that this, and the proposed amount, are acceptable to the organisers.

Arrange advertising

If pre-event programmes are being sent to competitors, make sure they advertise your sports massage service. This will save you a lot of work on the day of the event. Both the fee and the length of each massage need to be included in any advertisement.

Check the facilities

When contacting competition organisers, check what facilities will be available to you. In the UK, good weather can never be guaranteed, and athletes who have just endured a competitive event do not want to wait in cold, wet and windy conditions where

there is little shelter. Your potential clients are more likely to head for the nearest mode of transport home. Make sure you are offered reasonable shelter to work in, and, if the date happens to fall in a cold or wet season, make sure that there is shelter in a warm, dry building.

If you are sharing a tent or marquee, for example, check who else will be using the facility. Although you cannot always expect ideal conditions at sports events, it is advisable to be near the first aid organisation serving the event, and, equally, it is inadvisable to share facilities with other services such as catering, beer and entertainment. These attractions are often provided at non-competitive charity events; although they are great fun for the participants, they do not provide the best environment for effective sports massage.

Organise your equipment

Apart from the equipment already described in Chapter 2 and Appendix 2, it is advisable to take plenty of sports cologne and disposable tissues for cleaning the skin. The tissues may be used for removing the oil from the athlete's skin before they compete, or cleaning off mud and dirt afterwards. If you do not have access to water, the cologne will also serve to cleanse your hands in between massages. A nailbrush is also recommended to remove debris that collects under fingernails.

Arrange support personnel

If you are attending an event, try if possible to join a team of at least two or three people. Whether you are working in a team or working alone, take an extra person along – such as a friend or family member – who may be willing to usher competitors to your treatment area and organise a queue for you. This will relieve some of the pressures on you from athletes jostling for the next place on your massage couch. For the athletes, it provides the comfort of knowing that they have secured a place on a list. Athletes can also be advised on the waiting time so they can leave the queue, change and get some refreshments before returning in time to receive their massage. The person organising the queue will also be able to judge how many to allow in the queue. You obviously want to do all you can to please the athletes and avoid ending up with irate competitors who have been deprived of a massage after a long wait because the facilities are closing down.

If a large number of participants are expected at the event, try to work with other therapists. Again, this will relieve some of the pressure on you and make the event much more enjoyable.

◆ On the day ◆

When travelling to an event, allow plenty of time so that you are set up before you expect your first clients to arrive for a massage. This is important for your own wellbeing as much as that of the athletes. At many events, even those considered to be small-scale, there are often road closures and restricted areas that are marshalled by the organisers and the local police. If you arrive when the event is about to start, they may not allow you to pass through and you will end up having to take a much longer route. Extra walking while carrying your couch and other equipment will be particularly unwelcome and is not the best way to prepare for several hours massaging.

When you arrive, introduce yourself to the organisers and confirm the arrangements and the location for your sports massage service. After you have set up, contact other professionals on site such as first aiders, physiotherapists and doctors. If they have seen you setting up, they may be rather inquisitive as to what you are doing there. You should also check whether they would agree to client referrals – either to them or from them.

Depending on the venue and type of event you may need extra publicity when you get there. If announcements are being made over a loudspeaker system, make sure your sports massage service is one of them. Go and meet the competitors and tell them where your massage area is. And finally, don't forget to take plenty of your business cards or leaflets with you. You won't find a better opportunity to meet so many athletes who are so enthusiastic about sport – they may be potential long-term clients.

◆ How much can I earn? ◆

Don't expect to make a fortune from the event itself. However, you should at least cover your expenses and ideally make a small profit. As a qualified sports massage therapist you are entitled to charge for your service. Most competitors, from the elite athlete to the recreational runner, expect to pay a modest fee for an event massage, although much will depend on the sport and the type of event. Make sure you don't charge too much or competitors will be deterred from visiting your sports massage area. Although you may not gain much financially, your efforts may reap rewards when clients are encouraged to visit your practice later, having already sampled your skills at a sports event.

◆ Safety at sports events ◆

As a sports massage therapist you may also become involved in checking general safety and playing conditions at sports events. Some of the safety factors you may need to check are described below.

First aid officer

There should always be at least one person qualified in first aid (and preferably two or more, depending on the numbers attending) at every sports event. They deal with emergencies and carry out appropriate action if an injured player needs to go to hospital.

As a sports massage therapist you should be qualified in first aid if you are going to work at sports events. Make sure you gain a recognised qualification and attend a course that provides adequate training to equip you with the skills you may need. A short 'appointed persons' qualification will provide you with a first aid certificate, but will not teach you many of the basic first aid requirements.

The first aid officer is responsible for:

◆ finding the nearest telephone and making sure it works and is accessible at all times;
◆ finding out the location of the nearest hospital, and checking that it has a casualty department that is open at all times;
◆ ensuring that any personal medication given to them by players, such as inhalers or glucose tablets, is clearly labelled;
◆ ensure that access is available for an ambulance to reach the playing area, and this access is not obstructed during the event;
◆ finding the first aid kit and ensuring that there is access to it at all times. Before the day of the event, the contents should be checked to make sure it is equipped with all the appropriate first aid materials;

◆ checking the condition and accessibility of the stretcher;
◆ ensuring that a supply of clean running water and towels are available for first aid purposes;
◆ locating a supply of ice, if possible;
◆ liaising with other officials including organisers, referees, coaches and doctors, to clarify working areas, responsibilities, procedures, etc.

Playing surfaces and equipment

Surface inspections should be carried out regularly at all sports venues to check for obstructions, sharp obstacles, etc. Anything that poses a safety risk should be removed or fixed as appropriate. If large areas need to be checked for sharp stones or glass, a team may be needed to assist and to ensure the job is done quickly and effectively.

Corner flags must be constructed of flexible and breakable material. Goals and other posts should be padded where possible. Boundaries on indoor and outdoor playing areas should be a sufficient distance away and made of the appropriate material. Surfaces used for landing on, such as mats for high jump and pole vault, should be regularly checked. Indoor surfaces should not be slippery. Lighting should be appropriate and safe.

Safety personnel

Whatever sport or distance is involved, competitions must be properly marshalled by well-informed and adequate numbers of race officials. Such events need enormous co-ordination in ensuring maximum safety for both competitors and spectators. Losing athletes because of poor marshalling may have dire consequences if accidents occur on unsafe and unplanned routes, particularly if they involve vehicles. Weather conditions may also have a strong influence over how a particular race or event should be marshalled.

Clothing

All protective equipment should comply with the accepted standards for the sport concerned. Gloves, knee pads, shin pads, etc. all need to be made from good quality materials that withstand the rigours of the game. Other equipment, such as helmets and boot studs, may require a kite mark to show they meet required safety standards. Clothing should be properly fitted and appropriate for the climate involved, and where necessary extra clothing should be available to help keep athletes warm before, between, and after events. It is especially important that other equipment such as mouth guards are properly fitted, as they may cause choking if dislodged.

Shoes must not be too worn, and should be of a design appropriate to the playing surface. This will promote comfort and absorb impact. Poor footwear not only causes blisters, it may also result in twisted ankles or knee injuries.

Refereeing

Referees need to be properly trained and advised by governing bodies to enable them to interpret the rules correctly and so add clarity and clear boundaries to those in the game. Rules in sport are often modified to make the competition safer for those participating.

Children

If no parent or guardian is present, you will need to ensure that a club official has a contact number for each child in the event of an emergency.

Environmental factors

Climate
Careful attention must be paid to the weather, and not only in unfamiliar environments. Unexpected and extreme weather conditions, even in the local area, can play havoc for the competitors, particularly in endurance events. The utmost care must be taken by event organisers to ensure that competitors can be safely accommodated in the event of extreme weather conditions. Inexperience and over-enthusiasm in such circumstances may result in illness and injuries.

Altitude
Athletes competing at varying altitudes must allow a sufficient period to acclimatise before an event. Moving to a higher altitude can decrease the maximum uptake of oxygen due to the change in atmospheric pressure. For most people, above 1500 m (4921 ft), the decline in maximal aerobic power is approximately 3 per cent for every 300 m; below 1500 m this effect is largely absent. This reduction in the oxygen supplied to the muscles may adversely affect performance by 4–8 per cent, depending on the duration and intensity of competition – a considerable disadvantage at the finish line!

Altitude sickness can affect anyone, regardless of age, state of health or fitness level. Sufficient time must be allowed for recovery before starting intensive training. Symptoms of altitude sickness include frontal headache, nausea, dizziness, breathlessness, disorientation and fatigue. Effects often last for some hours; if symptoms persist, consult a doctor.

Chapter 14

Tips for success

So far, this book has covered many aspects of the knowledge, training and practical experience that you will need as the cornerstone for a career in sports massage therapy. Here are some more points for you to consider with regard to the personal qualities that will help you succeed. Many of these are linked to the fact that for at least part of your full-time career in this field, you will be self-employed and therefore require particular qualities to build your business. This means that as well as everything else you have learned you will need to be a good manager, self-disciplined, resilient and so on.

♦ What personal skills do I ♦ need to become successful?

Communication

Effective communication skills are essential. You must be able to listen and draw information from your client, and motivate them to use sports massage by educating them in the benefits for their sports performance.

Patience and perseverance

Be patient with your clients and patient for results. Positive results will depend on the age of your client, their level of activity, the time devoted to a training programme, and the time it takes for soft tissue to respond to and show the benefits of a sports massage session or programme of treatment.

Enthusiasm

Always be enthusiastic, but realistic, about what you believe you and your client can achieve. This does not mean you must always be jovial, which can be inappropriate if someone is suffering as a result of their condition or their related poor performance.

Self-discipline

Whether you are working for an employer, a club or in your own clinic, you must manage yourself and take full responsibility for your actions. You must be punctual, well-prepared, well-presented, and ensure that each appointment finishes on time so that your next client is not kept waiting.

Self-motivation

As well as being able to motivate others you must also be self-motivated at all times. You will suffer setbacks: you may not get the results you expected; a client may criticise you unfairly. Clients sometimes fail to turn up for appointments, and no matter how busy you become, there are times when the number of appointments falls away. During these periods it will be important for you to remain positive and cheerful, and not to let this affect the way you behave and speak with other clients.

Determination

Whatever results you achieve, you must remain determined for your sake and that of your clients. Being successful requires effort and hard work, especially in the early stages of your career. This also applies to your aims for your clients.

♦ How can I improve? ♦

Keep on learning. Sports medicine is a vast and ever-changing field of study. The more experience you gain in sports massage therapy, the more you will need to learn to further your skills, to apply them in different areas of sport, and to apply them in different circumstances.

Keep on training. This may involve advancing your knowledge and skills in sports massage or branching into closely related skills such as PNF stretching, trigger point release, or other soft tissue manipulation skills. Most therapists soon discover their niche. Once you've established your area of interest, remain focused on your aim – some therapists become so multiskilled that there is never time to utilise all their talents for the benefit of the client.

Gain as much experience with your own clients as you can. Try and observe others, either through a work experience arrangement, or when working with other therapists. Be cautious about new methods. If you observe a new method that appears to bring success, there may be other factors to consider. See if it works with other clients before you adopt it as part of your massage technique.

Finally, set high standards for yourself. This will rub off on your clients and they will be impressed by your aims.

♦ How do I promote my ♦ skills?

Be prepared to give short talks to athletes about your skills and the benefits they bring. If you do not like public speaking, start with small groups, and keep the talks short. This will build confidence which, in turn, will bring you clients and increase your business. For many therapists, attending sports events can be a constant source of inspiration, confidence, and new clients. Chapter 13 contains detailed advice on how to make sure they reap great rewards for you.

Whatever you do to promote yourself and the benefits of sports massage, don't oversell it. Emphasise the benefits of sports massage, but don't make false claims and don't be too forceful. A client may agree because they feel pressured, or they may worry that they will be pressured to attend further massage sessions. Clients will usually come to you because they have met you and listened to the benefits, or because someone else has recommended you.

♦ How do I develop ♦ my career?

Once you have a good idea of the area of sports and fitness in which you would like to work, try to meet other people working in the same field – not necessarily sports massage therapists – to find out the best ways to become involved and develop contacts.

Set goals which represent a series of small steps that will help you to achieve your main goal. There is no point in setting a goal of running your own full-time practice in two years without looking at the smaller steps you'll have to take to get there. This may seem like a daunting task, so keep it simple and make sure you set yourself small goals to achieve, say every three months, and this will make your main goal seem achievable. In this way, each small success will seem like another building block and will motivate you to the next step.

Keep a cool business head. Don't rush into every opportunity going or you may spend too much time doing poorly paid work in the hope of generating something more rewarding. Sometimes this does work, but you must set a value on your time and skills that should equate to what you need to earn a reasonable living. Your work will be more enjoyable if you are not under severe financial pressures.

Just as with any new career, it is a good idea to make a plan that summarises your goals and financial expectations. This will help you to monitor your progress and develop your career strategy as you proceed. Do not hesitate to seek professional advice when you need it.

Being a sports massage therapist requires persistent effort and personal development. Whether part-time or full-time, working in the profession will continue to inspire you, provide you with a lot of fun, and be tremendously satisfying.

Appendix 1

The massage couch

What should I look for when purchasing a portable massage couch?

When purchasing a portable couch it is advisable to obtain one at a height which best suits you. In addition, to gauge what is the correct height you must bear in mind that the shape and size of your clients will vary considerably – and therefore you may have to consider what will be best for massaging an average-sized person on your couch. It is also not worth spending extra money on adjustable-height couches, as you will rarely have the time – either in a clinic situation or at a sports event – to carry out any adjustment to your couch between sessions. The only circumstances in which you may need a couch of this type is if you are sharing it with other therapists; each of you will then adjust its height before your session starts. Bear in mind that adjustable legs are likely to raise the cost of your purchase considerably.

The base of your couch should ideally be constructed from hardwood, being the strongest and most lightweight of appropriate woods. The legs may also be constructed from hardwood, although anodised aluminium with cross-brace supports is recommended: these are likely to last much longer. There are normally four pairs of legs, with the centre two pairs interlocked and hinged so as to open out automatically as the couch is unfolded.

There should be adequate depth of padding on the top – 1.5 inches is quite sufficient. Any more than this begins to make the couch somewhat bulky. The padding should ideally be covered with vinyl so that the surface can be cleaned and dried quickly. In addition, it is recommended to purchase a couch with a facehole which will allow you to place your client in the best position (when lying prone) for massage of the neck and shoulders.

There are varying widths of massage couches which may be purchased, usually from 24 inches upwards. You will find the 24-inch width quite adequate for almost all individuals; wider couches may involve the therapist in having to stretch too much.

Figure A1 shows a typical portable massage couch, including facehole.

Figure A1 A typical massage couch

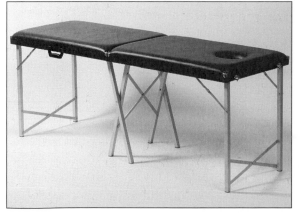

The treatment room

Once you have completed your practical training, you will require the following equipment in your treatment room. Bear in mind that you are likely to be travelling to sports events, so try to make sure that your equipment is lightweight and portable.

♦ Portable massage couch ♦

It may be quite feasible to own a robust and permanently-based massage couch in your treatment room. However, if you intend working in sport, you are almost certain to have to travel to sports venues, either for teams or for individual clients. It is therefore important that you purchase a well-constructed, portable couch which folds in half. In addition, you should possess a tough and durable carrying case to protect your investment from damage during transit. *See* also Appendix 1, for further information on purchasing a suitable massage couch.

♦ Bath sheet and towelling ♦ cover

You will require at least two bath-sized towels, one of which may be used folded and rolled to support your client behind the knees in the supine position, and under the ankles in the prone position (*see* also p. 87). The other

may be used to cover your client both for modesty and warmth. It is important to use bath-sized towels, as smaller towels often prove inadequate for such purposes.

You may also wish to keep a pillow or a third bath towel to support your client's head when they are lying in the supine position. Some form of covering for the couch is required: the best towelling covers available on the market have an elasticated edge which holds the cover in place.

In addition to this, while working in the field it is advisable to have with you a roll of tissue (to match the width of your couch) which you can put on your couch and dispose of between massage sessions. This is often necessary as you may be working with athletes who are muddy or, at the very least, perspiring.

♦ Flannels ♦

A supply of flannels is useful, particularly at sports venues. Sports cologne (*see* also pp. 8–9) may be placed on the flannel for the removal of oils; consequently the flannels become grubby quickly. Keep a number in reserve.

◆ Massage oils ◆

Last but not least, you will need plenty of massage oil and sports cologne. There are various forms of oil available and you will no doubt choose one to suit your own preference, and also that of your client. It is adviseable to buy the purest form of vegetable oil available, with little or no fragrance added, so reducing the possibility of any adverse skin reactions in your clients. Some essential oils may be added in very small quantities for general use, such as lavender and lemongrass which are known to be effective muscle relaxants. Any more substantial quantities will require you to undertake appropriate training in aromatherapy, as there are some contra-indications where essential oils may prove harmful. *See* Appendix 3 for more detail.

It is recommended to have sports cologne for removing any excess oil at the end of a massage session. Although most of the oil is usually absorbed into the skin, some clients like cologne to be used to ensure that no oil then rubs off on to their clothes. You may also find, particularly at events with large numbers of participants, that it is impossible for the organisers to provide washing or showering facilities, either for the athletes or the sports massage therapists. Sports cologne is ideal for removing any dirt from your client before massaging, and also for cleaning your own hands before massaging your next client.

Finally, when working in sport – and particularly in pre-competition situations – many athletes prefer not to have the oil left on when competing.

◆ Talcum powder ◆

Talcum powder has been widely used as a massage medium (although oils tend to be much preferred nowadays). It may be wise, therefore, to keep a small container of talc in case this is your client's preference. In some competitions, such as aerobics, the competitors are not allowed to appear with any form of oil on their skin.

◆ What about hygiene? ◆

As physical contact is the essence of sports massage, your appearance and personal hygiene are of the utmost importance. Hair should always be clean and tied back when necessary to avoid contact with the client. Special attention should be given to your hands; particular effort must be made to keep your nails short and your skin clean at all times. Hands should ideally be washed between treatment sessions (although when working in the field, this is not always possible). Again, sports cologne provides a very effective substitute for cleansing the hands before the next massage session.

◆ How should I prepare ◆ my treatment room?

When setting up a treatment room – whether as a permanent facility or a room for temporary use (such as within a sports club or leisure centre on an occasional basis) – the following principles apply.

◆ The room needs to be well ventilated and at the same time must have adequate means for providing warmth.

- All areas must be clean and preferably clear of other equipment and distractions.
- Ideally, the room should be situated near wash basins and a telephone, and a properly equipped first aid kit must be easily accessible.
- If you are using a room within a sports centre which has other uses during the rest of the week, suitable signs should be posted outside to indicate that this is a private treatment area.
- Finally, ice may be used during sports massage (*see* also p. 143) and therefore a ready supply in a nearby freezer or cool box is ideal.

♦ Tips to create a good ♦ impression

If the treatment room is a permanent facility, you will be required to display your qualifications, insurance cover and fees. Keep the room neat, tidy and clean. Some information charts on the walls relevant to your treatments will help if you need to communicate information more accurately to your client – but don't put too much up, or your clients may feel 'baffled by science'. It is often a good idea to mix the technical information with something more light-hearted, such as sports action photos. Remove as many other distractions from the room as possible, and make sure it is clearly indicated that your treatment room is private and should not be entered without knocking. The room itself should be kept warm but well ventilated. While it is nice to have a pleasant aroma in the room, do not laden the atmosphere too heavily with artificial fragrances. Often, the smell of the oils is quite sufficient.

Just as important as the room itself is your own appearance. Obviously, you must be smart and well dressed – but this must not be at the expense of your personal comfort. Sports massage can be hard work and you are likely to get warm. Therefore, even though you must create a good impression, it is quite acceptable to wear light clothing and training shoes. Hands must be clean, fingernails well trimmed, and hair kept tidy.

Finally, you must always be punctual and communicate well with all of your clients. To a large extent your success will depend on how effectively you relate to your clients.

Aromasport

Note: This section is intended merely as an introduction to the use of essential oils in sport. Although there are many benefits from their use, there may also be harmful side-effects to certain clients – for instance, during pregnancy. Therefore, an appropriate qualification must be obtained which will enable you to gain professional indemnity insurance (*see* also Chapter 2, p. 7) to prescribe and use essential oils for therapeutic effect.

◆ Do essential oils enhance ◆ the effects of sports massage?

Using aromatics for remedial effect in sport is nothing new. Thousands of years ago, Greek and Roman gladiators used perfumed ointments and powders lavishly to reduce fatigue, increase endurance and prepare for competition. The ancient Egyptians recognised their power too, and formulated 'perfumes-of-war' to instil feelings of aggression among the soldiers pre-battle. Essential oils were also highly prized for their medicinal action and many of these therapeutic applications – such as rosemary as an anti-inflammatory agent – are as relevant today as they were in antiquity.

Many civilisations have continued to see the value of these natural remedies, with each contributing their own plant recipes and prescriptions. Today, sports therapists can contribute some of their own.

◆ What is 'Aromasport'? ◆

Aromasport is a combination of the specific application of essential oils, with sports massage (and other methods of treatment where applicable), to achieve maximum therapeutic benefit during and after physical exercise.

This may be by aiming to enhance performance, aid recovery and thereby reduce possible harmful effects – such as suppression of the immune system; or by reducing the risk of injury by improving other factors such as the psychological condition of the athlete. The great thing about essential oils is that they are natural products. People participating in sports should always be wary of what they consume, since many 'off-the-shelf' products contain substances that are banned in sport and athletes therefore have to be careful. By contrast, essential oils can enhance the performance of athletes without many of the risks associated with other products.

◆ What are essential oils? ◆

Essential oils are whole, organic substances extracted from seeds, roots, stems, woods, leaves, fruits and flowers of aromatic plants. The chemical composition of essential oils is complex and further reading of more specialised books is recommended.

Each essential oil has its own unique characteristics and therapeutic qualities, but is generally healing, having antibiotic, anti-viral, antiseptic and anti-bacterial properties to some degree. All essential oils are:

♦ natural/drug-free;
♦ volatile (evaporate easily);
♦ aromatic;
♦ concentrated;
♦ lipophilic (soluble in skin grease);
♦ colourless (with a few exceptions);
♦ liquid (a few are semi-solid);
♦ inflammable;
♦ soluble in alcohol, semi-soluble in water.

♦ How do they work? ♦

Physiologically, essential oils penetrate right into the deep layers of our skin – moving from there to various organs, glands and tissues throughout the body. They are also taken up by the lymph fluid that provides moisture for every cell of the body, and may be absorbed when inhaled into the lungs, passing through the fine membrane and into the bloodstream.

The specific remedial action of essential oils depends on their individual therapeutic properties. The oils are highly aromatic, activating the sense of smell when they are inhaled; this can have a psychological, as well as a physical, effect. The act of rubbing the oils into the body using sports massage techniques, along with inhalation of the aroma, enables a greater level of absorption as the chemical compounds reach the blood-stream by passing through the skin and when breathed into the lungs.

Just as with sports massage itself, it is difficult to separate the physiological and psychological benefits of essential oils. It is in fact this dual action itself which may be used in sports therapy for maximum benefit!

♦ Can Aromasport be used for ♦ injury prevention?

Regular application of essential oils in conjunction with sports massage can assist in preventing injury by enhancing the effects of sports massage to maintain health and aid recovery. Thus, the athlete may achieve a more consistently healthy state of mind and body.

The following is a summary of the benefits of essential oils.

Maintains health

♦ Generally strengthens all systems of the body.
♦ Promotes healthy state of soft tissue.
♦ Balances the body according to need.
♦ Builds immunity and raises resistance to infection.
♦ Relieves stress and tension.
♦ Promotes positive attitude and mental wellbeing.

Aids recovery

♦ Relieves muscle tightness and spasm.
♦ Alleviates pain.
♦ Promotes healing.
♦ Soothes and reduces inflammation.
♦ Diminishs effects of fatigue (mind and body).
♦ Reduces effects of immune suppression often associated with heavy training/competition.

♦ Therapeutic properties of ♦ essential oils

Three distinct modes of action of essential oils have been recognised: *pharmacological* (causing chemical changes within the body), *physiological* (affecting specific body systems) and *psychological* (eliciting 'odour response').

It is important to note that the essential oil in its pure, natural state has been found to be more effective than its principal constituent. The antiseptic power of eucalyptus oil in its unadulterated form, for example, has been found to be stronger than its isolated main component, 'eucalyptol' (Cuthbert Hall, 1904*).

Each essential oil possesses several therapeutic properties and is thus capable of producing many different actions whether applied directly to the skin, or via inhalation. Such versatility means that several oils will produce the desired therapeutic effect, but also that one oil will prove effective for a variety of conditions. This is good news for the sports practitioner as it means a few, well-chosen oils can provide a myriad of uses!.

♦ What to consider when ♦ selecting oils

The aim must be to choose an appropriate oil or mix to give maximum benefit according to the needs of the individual (or group, if selecting oils for a 'team mix').

Your assessment should be based on your client's state of mind and body, and related to the environment, type of sport, and timing of the physical exercise – i.e., pre- or post-competition. Consideration must also be given to lifestyle, history, diet and gender.

*Cuthburt Hall (1904), in Arnold Taylor, W. E. (1984), *Phys-Essential Therapy: Armomatherapy for the Whole Person* (Cheltenham: Stanley Thornes), p. 16 .

Pre- or post-competition?

Pre-competition mixes will tend to be stimulating and strengthening. (However, relaxing and calming oils used to massage the neck and shoulders would be more appropriate for an overanxious competitor). Post-competition mixes will aim to relax and promote recovery.

Once an assessment has been made, oil(s) should be chosen for their specific therapeutic properties. Remember, the aroma should be pleasing to the recipient in order to be of positive benefit – i.e., if it smells good, it does good! Also, each person is unique and so experimentation is encouraged and other oil options may be required.

♦ Is there a 'psycho-aromatic' ♦ influence on athletes?

It is generally accepted that the mental state of an athlete has a profound influence on their performance. Sports psychology is big business today, and techniques to develop mental preparation – the 'winning mind' – are now commonplace in top-level sport.

So, can aromatic oils play a significant part in this process, by influencing mood and attitude during training and competition by activating the olfactory senses? Further research is needed in this area to study the effects of odours of essential oils on performance in sport, before this question can fully be answered. However, research and experimentation is currently underway to determine which aromas are most effective, within realistic limits, to:

♦ promote positive attitude and boost confidence;
♦ stimulate arousal and create an attacking mood;

- reduce performance anxiety, tension and mental fatigue;
- aid concentration and memory;
- induce relaxation (especially if over-stimulated);
- counteract depression (poor performance, injury/trauma).

◆ Best methods of using ◆ essential oils

The use of essential oils may not be well received by all athletes – especially some of the pleasant aromas in a normally aggressive environment! Sometimes, more subtle methods of using essential oils may be adopted for the benefit of the athlete(s) so that they are unaware of them but still benefit. Here are just a few ideas of different methods of application.

- Through Sports massage applied by a practitioner, or self-administered.
- Inhalation – perhaps the most direct and convenient method. For example, a few drops of oil on a tissue (ensure that the oil does not come into contact with the skin), or sprayed into the atmosphere via a spray bottle.
- Vaporisation is ideal for dressing rooms, training areas and treatment rooms.
- Via an electrical diffuser or candle burner.
- Bath – self-treatment method. Useful if massage is not possible or contraindicated, and to encourage self-treatment at home.

◆ Can oils help to reduce ◆ immune system suppression?

Essential oils have played a significant part throughout history in helping to protect the human body against disease and contagion. They are known to possess anti-viral and bacteriostatic properties, which are as relevant today as they were in the past.

As well as these traditionally accepted effects, it is suggested that essential oils have a powerful immune-strengthening potential, which can be used in sports therapy to great benefit. Little is known about the precise working of the immune system, but recent research has shown that intense exercise has dramatic effect on immunity and depletes the body's natural defences.

Experimental work by Dr Lynn Fitzgerald* has suggested that by pushing the body to the limit through exercise, the ability to fight infection is reduced. Dr Fitzgerald emphasises that it is not just elite athletes who are susceptible to this immune depression; anyone who trains hard is vulnerable. It is worth noting that Dr Fitzgerald has highlighted the most critical period for infection as being up to 20 hours after a vigorous training session or competition.

Careful and regular application of essential oils via massage, baths, inhalation and vaporisation (*see* above) can help to reinforce the body's defence mechanism. This provides a potent force to help reduce the threat of recurring infections that often plague those that train regularly. The oils represent a useful alternative to commercial cold and flu remedies, many of which are high on the IOC 'Banned List of Substances'.

Regular use is recommended to build immunity and fight infection, with regard to periods following competition or hard training, sports with a high risk of infection such as open water swimming, close contact

---

*Fitzgerald, L. (1991), 'Overtraining increases the susceptibility to infection', *International Journal of Sports Medicine*, **12**(1), pp. 5–8.
— (1994), 'Exercise and the immune system', NSMI Evening Lecture Series.

team sports (e.g. rugby) and endurance sports (e.g. marathon running).

◆ How can Aromasport be ◆ used in the first aid kit?

There are many possible uses for essential oils, not only for the healthy athlete, but also in the first aid situation. Here are some uses that have been found to be effective.

◆ Cleansing agents. Some oils such as lavender and lemon, may be used as cleansing agents. You may add a total of 20–30 drops to 100 ml purified water, and apply using a spray gun so that there is no risk of contaminated fluid getting back into the container.
◆ 'Hot and Cold' contrast baths. Five drops each of rosemary and lavender may be added to each bowl of water when using Hot and Cold contrast baths.
◆ Skin applications. Lavender may be used neat or diluted for minor cuts, grazes, blisters, rashes, burns, sunburn, chapping, insect bites, headache, fainting, dizziness and exhaustion.
◆ Sports massage oil/lotion. For general treatment of aches, pains, cramp and stiffness, try lavender, marjoram, roman chamomile, black pepper and arnica in 1–2 per cent dilution in a base oil or lotion.
◆ Bruise remedy. Apply arnica cream or oil to a bruise, or try a cold compress with a few drops of geranium on gauze dampened with witchazel and attach with micropore. (*Caution:* large bruises may indicate a fracture – refer for X-ray!).
◆ Use friars balsam to seal edges of a wound and cracks in heels.
◆ Skin protection. Lavender or tea tree added to vaseline for cuts on eyebrows, face, grass burns; use as chapping ointment and pre-ice barrier.

◆ Can Aromasport help ◆ rehabilitation from injuries

Sports injuries are an inevitable occurrence for some people who participate in sport. The main concern of the sport massage therapist is to refer for diagnosis when necessary, and help the injured athlete return to their sport as safely and as soon as possible.

Application of essential oils can generally assist in the treatment of and recovery from injury by increasing the effectiveness of therapeutic modalities. Some of these treatments have been mentioned for first aid (*see* above). The same uses, such as hot and cold treatment, may in some instances be continued throughout the rehabilitation programme. Localised massage, or gentle application of oils to an injury site or adjacent area, is encouraged.

While helping to restore function, essential oils also act to:

◆ assist healing and regeneration;
◆ strengthen and re-balance;
◆ promote relaxation;
◆ reduce negative mental attitude/mood often associated with injury (depression, anxiety, lethargy, low self-esteem).

Aromasport treatments provide an ideal way to encourage self-help via home treatments that can be tailor-made to suit the needs of the individual (massage, baths, inhalation/vaporisation, use of creams and ointments, etc.).

Finally, you owe it to yourself and your clients to purchase only the best quality pure essential oils for therapeutic use. Price is a key to the quality of an oil and it is important to buy from reputable suppliers who carry out regular checks on the quality of their oils.

Note: Thanks to Stephanie Coxton for providing the information contained in this chapter.

Recommended reading

Anatomy Palpation and Surface Markings (2nd ed.), Derek Field (London: Butterworth Heinemann, 1997)

Aromatherapy and the Mind, Julia Lawless (London: Thorsons, 1994)

Beard's Massage (4th ed.), Giovanni de Domenico and Elizabeth C. Woods (London: W.B. Saunders & Co. Ltd, 1997)

The Complete Guide to Strength Training, Anita Bean (London: A & C Black, 1998)

The Complete Guide to Stretching, Christopher M. Norris (London: A & C Black, 1999)

Fitness and Health (4th ed.) Brian J. Sharkey (Champaign, Illinois: Human Kinetics, 1997)

Palpation Skills, Leon Chaitow (New York: Churchill Livingstone, 1997)

Physiology and Sport & Exercise, J. H. Wilmore and D. L. Costill (Champaign, Illinois: Human Kinetics, 1994)

Principles of Human Anatomy (8th ed.), Gerard Tortora (London: HarperCollins, 1996)

Science of Flexibility (2nd ed.), Michael J. Alter (Champaign, Illinois: Human Kinetics, 1988)

Soft Tissue Injuries in Sport (2nd ed.), Sylvia Lachmann and John R. Jenner (Oxford: Blackwell Scientific Publications, 1994)

Therapeutic Massage, Elizabeth Holey and Eileen Cook (London: W.B. Saunders & Co. Ltd, 1997)

Useful contacts

The Academy of Sports Therapy
29A Mill Lane
Welwyn
Herts AL6 9EU
Tel: 01438 717374
Website: www.sportstherapy.co.uk

Independent Professional Therapists
   International
St Michael's Place
58A Bridgegate
Retford
Notts DN22 7UZ
Tel: 01777 700383
Email: iptiuk@aol.com

National Sports Medicine Insitute of the
   United Kingdom
c/o Medical College of St Bartholomew's
   Hospital
Charterhouse Square
London EC1M 6BQ
Tel: 020-7251 0583
Website: www.nsmi.org.uk

The National Training Organisation for
   Sport Recreation & Allied Occupations
24 Stephenson Way
London NW1 2DH
Tel: 020-7388 7755
Email: the.nto@sprito.org.uk

Sport England
Information Centre
16 Upper Woburn Place
London WC1H 0QP
Tel: 020-7273 1500
Website: www.english.sports.gov.uk

Index

Note: italic entries refer to illustrations

MANNA FROM HADES

MANNA
FROM HADES

A Cornish Mystery

CAROLA DUNN

CRIME

Constable & Robinson Ltd
55–56 Russell Square
London WC1B 4HP
www.constablerobinson.com

First published in the US by Minotaur Books,
an imprint of St Martin's Publishing Group, New York, 2009

First published in the UK by C&R Crime,
an imprint of Constable & Robinson, 2013

A copy of the British Library Cataloguing in Publication
Data is available from the British Library

ISBN 978-1-78033-648-0 (paperback)
ISBN 978-1-47210-479-3 (ebook)

Printed and bound in the UK

1 3 5 7 9 10 8 6 4 2

In memory of my godmother, Bet (Beatrice Helen Jellinek), to whom I owe many happy holidays in Cornwall—and so much more.

Also, many thanks for all their help and support, above and beyond the call of duty, to my "full-service" agent, Alice Volpe, Northwest Literary Agency, Inc., and to Alan and Slick.